This map was prepared from information courtesy of
ST. LAWRENCE SEAWAY DEVELOPMENT CORPORATION, Corp of Engineers U.S. Army
by Robert Topor and Ed Fisher, Jr. 1957

T4-AJS-265

THE NEW ST. LAWRENCE FRONTIER

THE NEW ST. LAWRENCE FRONTIER

*A survey of the economic
potential in the St. Lawrence
area of New York State
by*
Sidney C. Sufrin
and
Edward E. Palmer

Maxwell School Series / Syracuse University Press

Library of Congress Catalog Card Number: 57-12961

© 1957, SYRACUSE UNIVERSITY PRESS

338.97
S946n

To Grace and Mudge

*Behold, I have set before you an open
door, which no one is able to shut.*

REVELATION, 3:8

247917

PREFACE

The United States and Canada are engaged in a joint project which will more effectively link the trade and industry of North America to the trade and industry of the world. The Seaway from the Great Lakes to the Atlantic Ocean, by being deepened and widened, converts the Great Lakes ports to ocean ports. The Power Project at Massena, New York, for its part, will have an enormous impact in the local area and a considerable impact in the larger region of the St. Lawrence Valley.

Within the next few years these projects will have caused the expenditure of at least a billion dollars. Before the new facilities are brought into use many more millions will have been spent in housing, docks, harbors, and industrial and business facilities. Economic theory and experience teach us that such great expenditures will have great and, in the main, beneficial effects on the economic development of the American and Canadian areas where the money is spent.

But the Seaway and the Power Project are more

than local public works. The great wheatlands of the United States and Canada will gain access to world markets which high transportation costs have made prohibitive prior to the present development. The Seaway, if it opens new markets to North American agriculture, might very well help solve the hunger problem of the world and the United States-Canadian farm problem. Furthermore, an era of intensive agriculture might be introduced into the traditionally extensive farm culture of the Great Plains. Industry of the Middle West and of Canada's industrial belt, too, may find a rich stimulus and new orientation because of the Seaway and cheap water transport.

The analogy between the Erie Canal and the Seaway comes to mind almost automatically. The whole of the United States benefited from the Canal. Some cities, some industries, some regions gained more than others but on the whole the Erie Canal raised the tone of the *entire* economic system. In relative terms the Seaway will surely not have so magnificent an effect as had the old Erie Canal. The sheer size and complexity of the modern American economic system rule this out. Nevertheless, in absolute terms the Seaway has the potential of playing an important economic and defense role in United States-Canadian development.

An appreciable fraction of the Seaway expenditure and virtually all of the power plant expenditure will be in the area around Massena. New York's St. Lawrence Valley is industrially undeveloped. Yet it lies close to the major industrial axes of Canada and the United States. This study examines in some detail the economic potential of the St. Lawrence Valley and offers what we hope are constructive suggestions for its development.

Before the passage of the St. Lawrence Seaway

Act by the Congress in 1954, and, to a greater extent, since its passage, there has been a great deal of talk about the future "North Country" of New York State and its potential contribution to the American economy. Most of the talk, however, has been speculative and based on little more than hearsay and extravagances of ignorance.

Four Syracuse University professors, in 1955-56, supervised the examination by graduate students of the setting and possible impact of the St. Lawrence Valley development to clarify at least their own thinking. Drs. Robert E. Dickinson and John Thompson, of the University's Geography Department, each directed studies generally concerned with the economic resources and existing urban, rural, and transport structure of the area; and Drs. A. M. McIsaac and Jesse Burkhead, of the Economics Department, directed the examination of some aspects of the economic and investment potential of the area.

One of the present writers had the opportunity to consult with the directors of the four "staff papers" while the work was in progress. Some of the basic materials of the four reports provide important data for the present analysis, but, in addition, other sources have been used freely. Obviously none of the professional researchers who directed the basic investigations are responsible for the opinions or analyses of this present study, although each of the reports has been substantively helpful.

It is hoped that at least four different groups may benefit and be stimulated by this exposition: *first*, those who live, or intend to take up residence, in the St. Lawrence area itself; *second*, those who are connected with the policies and administration of businesses located in the area, or that might contemplate moving there; *third*, the numerous officers and employees of the various local, state, and federal agencies which are concerned with public welfare generally; and *fourth,* those in other areas who may be interested in any large economic development in the American economy.

The St. Lawrence Valley is not a vast expanse; but neither is it tiny. It covers an approximate 4,000 square miles and is heterogeneous in character. The 200,000 people living in the area are dispersed unevenly, with about half of them living in rural environs and the other half in urban centers. Most of the urban communities of the Valley are small when compared with other urban centers of the state. There is a wide variety of resources and a great inconsistency in the degree to which the various parts of the area are developed. There are, of course, common characteristics running throughout the area, but for the most part it is a territory distinguished by its diversity. The development of the St. Lawrence Seaway and the construction of the Power Project are certain to affect the whole area; and since they introduce new elements into the life of the community, they will just as certainly give it a new or at least modified impetus and orientation. It is reasonable to suppose, therefore, that any progress toward common knowledge of the area on the part of those living in it will be a decided gain. Both public and semipublic institutions, such as civic organizations, clubs, Chambers of Commerce, business corporations, and banking, credit, and other commercial institutions may well profit by a fresh, new, mutual, and harmonious understanding of the community in which they operate.

America is a growing society. In this dynamic land even resources are far from static. Population, income, technology, services, and problems are expanding. Business activity is growing in the present years more than ever before.

What is more, new businesses are continually being formed. Those who are potential business investors and business architects quite properly wish to consider carefully all possible locations in the United States before choosing a particular site. Yet it is probably true that there is much that is not learned by the potential investor about many of the areas that may be under consideration, or, for that matter, even about the area that may eventually be chosen. The investor only knows what is available for him to discover. It is hoped that such a study as this may present additional knowledge to such persons, who may not be able to attain the information elsewhere.

There are a considerable number of local, state and federal agencies concerned, by their very nature, with public welfare; and many of these, by their special jurisdictions, are particularly concerned with what is to happen in the St. Lawrence area. The interest of these agencies is broad, and includes national defense, industrial development and production, transportation, housing, health, education, and many other elements affecting the general well-being of the people. The accurate formulation of problems in the St. Lawrence region, the nature of the problems and their possible solution or resolution are certainly of major interest to every level and every agency of government which has valid interests in the way of life, the institutions, and the people of the St. Lawrence area.

The authors share a hope that there are many persons living in other and even far distant parts of the United States and the world at large who are motivated by a wonderful curiosity to know more and more about every part of the world in which they live. This little book is also meant for them.

CONTENTS

THE ST. LAWRENCE
FRONTIER

The twentieth century, with a depression sandwiched between two World Wars, has been a time of frustration and
disillusionment for mankind. Nevertheless, the twentieth
century has also been a period of great artistic, social, industrial, and political development in the western world.
We are torn between a feeling, on the one hand, that all is
lost and, on the other, that a great future of happiness awaits
us. The optimism traditionally associated with America has
suffered some setbacks, but it is not defeated. Americans
see the world changing before their very eyes. They see
their own society changing, too. But they are apprehensive
as to what the change will be like: the future is not envisioned so clearly as it was even two or three generations
ago. Nor is there such superb confidence in their own youth,
and in progress: Americans have grown up, and many of
their hopes and aspirations have either been achieved or
have been dissolved in the great heat of American life.

1

If this be an accurate statement of what is happening to American optimism, there is some evidence to support it. Optimism sleeps! For many, the spirited enthusiasm with which eighteenth- and nineteenth-century Americans went about the task of developing a nation has waned. Whereas the many early citizens used to look at the countryside with the exhilaration of those who have discovered a treasure, more than a few now view it with a sense of indifference. They still claim the predilection for democracy, but they lack the motivation that breeds the dynamism on which the free democratic society thrives.

Perhaps one of the main reasons for a change of heart and a change of attitude among Americans, if indeed such changes are real and not imaginary, is that science and technology have brought the rest of the world—for the most part a suppressed and deprived world—so close in terms of transportation and communication that Americans have become unable to identify the possibilities for further development at home, and have become obsessed with the problem of having to devote American resources and enterprise to making older societies tolerable and decent.

The world is not yet perfect. That fact is easily recognized. Nor has America yet reached perfection, and to continue its development may never bring the millennium. But to refuse to continue to discover and meet new challenges with enthusiasm, to progress at home, to improve and ameliorate other societies in foreign lands is refusal, we hope, that is based merely on passing public fancy. Greater possibilities lie ahead for the improvement and the enrichment of human life both at home and abroad.

It has been said that the character of the mind and institutions of America were determined during the late eighteenth and nineteenth centuries by the existence of a great land frontier; and that the closing of our frontier at about the turn into the twentieth century terminated the development of uniquely American institutions. Since the development of such institutions was so perfectly in tune with the American spirit, it is sometimes claimed that the disappearance of the frontier desiccated American optimism.

The irony and inaccuracy of all this is that bona fide frontiers still exist in America. They are not the geographical frontier of the open West, but they are nonetheless genuine; and America abounds in them. With the recent development of our foreign aid programs, American citizens have become thoroughly aware of the great problems and the fantastic needs of the vast underprivileged areas of other continents. But because these have been called "underdeveloped" areas, and because many of them are, at the present time, undesirable places in which to live, the whole concept of "underdeveloped places" has come to mean "undesirable" and "underprivileged" areas. What is more, they have come to be thought of as far-away places seldom visited by Americans.

A far more accurate use of the term "underdevelopment" refers to an area, or region, or community which has not organized itself for the maximum use of its resources. Neither the human nor the natural resources of the special place referred to are being utilized in such a way as to create as rich and full a life for its people as the proper development and use of those resources could reasonably make possible. Such places as these are the truly underdeveloped areas — and they are the frontiers!

During the 1930's it became clear to most people of this country, the richest in the world, that there were

3

large areas of underdevelopment in the United States. There were rich resources in these places, but they had never been tapped, organized, or utilized. The development of the Tennessee Valley, with all its various implications, stands out as a dramatic example of what can happen when such underdeveloped areas — such frontiers — are met with fruitful imaginations. Here the government played a leading role. In other cases, such as in the industrial development of California and the other southwestern states, private industry took the lead, with help from local and state governments. Development of this type is not a restricted province. States, the federal government, and private capital all can and do play important roles.

New York is commonly thought of, and with adequate justification, as the richest state of all. This does not mean that the use of every index will find New York the number one state, but, generally speaking, it is considered among the most productive and fully developed of the United States. If New Yorkers feel too smug about these generalizations, however, such pride as they do experience may possibly be damaged when they cease thinking in terms of measures for the state as a whole; for there are great discrepancies in the level of living in some parts of the state as compared to others.

In the field of agriculture, for example, New York is highly prosperous and highly developed. Though much less desirable land has been taken out of production, and thus the number of farms has declined by almost 50 per cent in the last century, the increase in average size of farms has been over 25 per cent; over-all agricultural production has approximately doubled; and productivity per agricultural worker has more than tripled. Further, the agricultural economy of the state has become highly diversified. Though not nearly the largest in area of the forty-eight states, New York is second to none but Wisconsin in milk and dairy products, is third and fifth respectively in vegetable and fruit production, and it ranks among the top three states in the country in the production of over a dozen important farm products.

This generally favorable picture, however, masks the wide differentials between areas within the state. In 1950, of the 135,000 to 140,000 rural farm families in the state, 20 per cent had incomes of less than $1,000 and 40 per cent had less than $2,000. Such discrepancies are not, moreover, peculiar to the functional area of agriculture but are equaled, if not surpassed, in conservation, education, health, housing, and industrial development.

Perhaps the most thoroughly underdeveloped area in New York State is that geographic tract which is commonly referred to as the St. Lawrence area, for it is indeed an area in which the full potential in its natural and human resources has never been approached. In this sense the area is one of the great frontiers of the state and the region. But it is particularly a frontier for American industrial expansion.

The characterization of any area as a frontier usually implies that it is on the edge of civilization, or at least beyond the geographical limits or boundaries of intensive agriculture, trade, and industry. But there are different kinds of frontiers; land, free land, is not a necessary component in the concept at all. There are intellectual, social, scientific, political, and certainly *economic* frontiers, none of which is necessarily so closely related to geographic or land factors.

This is particularly true of much present-day economic activity. Economic frontiers extend throughout technology and the process of capital use. They permeate the problem of resource utilization and the way in which human beings are organized or organize themselves for living.

A vast new resource is now being developed on the United States-Canadian border; and much of this development is taking place within New York State. This new resource is the St. Lawrence Seaway and the Barnhart Island Power Project. The two projects make up one of the greatest single technological undertakings being developed on the North American continent. The construction, already well under way, will soon transform the International Rapids section of the St. Lawrence River at Massena, New York, into a mighty source of electrical energy. And, further, it will create a new and extremely important and invaluable artery of international trade and commerce.

The Seaway and the power development are being carried out as a cooperative venture by the United States and Canada. They are likely to involve an expenditure of over one billion dollars when completed. The two national governments are to expend an estimated $300,000,000 in the modernization of navigation facilities, while the Power Project, the cost of which is estimated presently at $600,-000,000, is being developed jointly by the Hydro-Electric Power Commission of Ontario and the state of New York. It is intended that the Seaway will be completed in the year of 1959 and, when it is finished, it will provide a 27-foot channel between Montreal and the Great Lakes. The output from the Power Project, however, is scheduled to become available for use in 1958. The installation will produce a maximum of about two million kilowatt-hours, an output almost equal to that of the Grand Coulee Dam in the state of Washington. Thus the Barnhart Island Power Project will

6

become one of the largest hydroelectric installations in the world.

The power output will be shared equally between the United States and Canada. The main source of production will be a 3,500-foot powerhouse, the longest structure of its kind in the world, to be constructed between Barnhart Island and Canada. This massive physical structure will span the river and create a lake over 30 miles long and 4 to 5 miles wide. The international boundary between Canada and America will bisect the installation.

It is thoroughly obvious that there is ample opportunity here to develop new and fruitful procedures, policies, and methods in international and intergovernmental cooperation for economic programing and development. And it is just as clear that the industrial factors of technology, population, and new resources are provided and present, though the full complement of capital has still to be secured to facilitate the optimum use of those economic factors that are already at hand. This is a field for both public and private action on a grand scale.

Any appraisal or reappraisal of the St. Lawrence area and its potential for economic development cannot but be an inspirited, exhilarating one, for the area comprises the part of New York State immediately adjacent to the Seaway and Power Projects.

Though the area lies within the counties of Jefferson, St. Lawrence, and Franklin, our interest is not focused on the whole of the three counties. To be sure, they each lie next to the St. Lawrence River, but they also stretch far inland and up into the Adirondack highlands. Jefferson County falls completely within the particular area with which we are directly concerned. The other two counties, however, lie only partially in the area between the highlands and the river. The St. Lawrence area as it is defined here, then, refers to a belt of land, 25 to 30 miles wide, lying between the Adirondack Mountains and the St. Lawrence River. Perhaps a convenient mountainside boundary might be located at the beginning of the Adirondack State Park. The belt includes about two-thirds of the area of the three counties, but nearly five-sixths of their 230,000 population.

Many people who perhaps have never visited the St. Lawrence area of New York State have nonetheless become familiar with the Paul Bunyan-like tales that have been accumulating for decades about its physical characteristics. The entire area is frequently described and pictured as a rugged, mountainous, and severe region; an isolated place of wilderness and heavy forests. The winters are often referred to as extremely cold, filled with ice and snow, with the thermometer lingering for most of the winter months around 20 to 25 degrees below zero. Some have gone so far as to describe the year there as "360 days of winter—and 5 days of slush." The people in the area are often characterized as an uneducated, backward stock, unsophisticated, though showing flashes of a kind of raw Yankee wit and wisdom— a people whose major vocations are fishing, trapping, hunting, and trading with the Indians.

Every section in the country has its folklore, and the St. Lawrence area is certainly no exception. There is always a theme of humor in these legendary fabrications— but they are mammoth exaggerations. If they contain any truth at all, it is not more than a small grain or two. The view of the St. Lawrence area represented in them is certainly not based in fact, for the area is not mountainous, nor heavily forested, nor are its people primarily hunters, trap-

8

pers, fur-traders, and fishermen. And the Indian has long since disappeared. As for the weather, the snowfall averages about 80 inches a year, which does not exceed the normal fall at points much further south in New York State. Degree-days[1] range between 8,000 and 9,000 annually. And when one brings to mind that the area is richly endowed with institutions of higher learning, the idea that the area is "backwoods" in character is completely exploded.

The almost unlimited possibilities of the St. Lawrence area may be more easily envisioned if one views it in a broader geographical context. It lies about halfway between the great population areas of "upstate" New York, that is, Schenectady, Albany, Utica, Syracuse, Rochester, and Buffalo, on the one hand, and the great population belt of Canada, in which is included the Montreal-Toronto industrial axis, on the other. A moderately well-developed network of roads and railroads, in addition to commercial airline routes, provides abundant connection to the industry and commerce of Canada and provides ready entry into the New York City-Chicago industrial axis, the present northern boundaries of which are just slightly to the south of the St. Lawrence area. The industrial East and the Middle West and Prairie Provinces are already connected by a water route, but the establishment of the Seaway will provide its full development. Moreover, the Seaway's construction will create and furnish the St. Lawrence area with an excellent connection with the whole wide world, for it does indeed bring the Great Lakes to the Atlantic Ocean and makes seaports of lakeports.

---

[1]Degree-days are the sum of the differences between the high and low daily average temperatures subtracted from 65 degrees.

9

Here, then, in the St. Lawrence area, is a wonderfully genuine frontier. Yet it is not on the periphery of civilization. It is in the very center! All the long travail of frontier development, as we picture it in early American experience, is largely completed. Here is a frontier with practically all the pain, misery, sweat, tears, and tribulation extracted. It already possesses most of the public and private investments, most of the public utilities, most of the schools, hospitals, roads, and communication facilities, all of which are so extremely costly for any newly developing area to secure. Thus it would seem to be an industrial and business frontier made to order. Just how much economic potential is there in the St. Lawrence area? Is it the "found" horizon it appears to be? That is the question we shall try to answer.

THE LIVING
ECONOMIC COMMUNITY

In a dynamic, changing world the future of any area is never very clearly seen. It is thus extremely difficult to play the part of the prophet by advancing quantitative predictions. At the very best, one can only define the most likely directions in which a community may develop, and these directions may be defined validly in terms of qualitative appraisals only. Our main concern, then, is to analyze both the nature and the apparent directions of growth; but we shall also be interested in the character and strength of the probable obstacles to such growth.

If the ultimate concern is to analyze and suggest the various general patterns which change can and probably will assume in the foreseeable future, it will most certainly facilitate such an analysis to examine at the very first the St. Lawrence area as a living community.

Were one to examine carefully the past history and present setting of the St. Lawrence, or, for that matter, any other region in the United States, such an examination might

11

not contribute any clearly valid insight into what may be in store in the immediate or distant future. As we have stated, a new factor has been added to the community life of the St. Lawrence area; a new resource is being created. The navigational improvements, both planned and now actually being consummated by the American and Canadian governments, and the construction of a gigantic power installation at Barnhart Island by the province of Ontario and New York State will provide a powerful impetus to the economic and social life in the area. It would have been difficult to foretell accurately the changes that were to be brought about by such great projects as the Grand Coulee Dam, the Tennessee Valley development, or even the Erie Canal. And it must be remembered that each of these three undertakings precipitated a far-reaching and fundamental change in the very nature of the regions affected. The establishment of the Seaway and the building of the Power Project in northern New York could as well revolutionize the whole economic nature and structure of the St. Lawrence area. Thus the history or setting of a community may not always be considered as a reliable guide to the future, and this is very likely to be true of the area we are describing. However, some kind of an inventory of the endowments of the area may be necessary or at least helpful as a starting place for making estimates as to the future.

Much of the St. Lawrence area is devoted to agriculture, and it is an important dairy farm section of New York State. A good look at any road map of the state will disclose, however, that there is a major resource that is largely undeveloped in the area—a resource the development of which not only enhances but is actually necessary to the prosperity of a dairy community. There is no uniform system of good roadways. Such a situation imposes a great burden on the further development of the dairy industry. Easy access to milk depots and other market channels is not available for the dairy farmers, and there is a great need for such a system.

The land, on the other hand, is generally well suited for the dairy industry. It is a loamy, undulating, rolling land and extends over large parts of both St. Lawrence and Franklin Counties. Jefferson County is an exception, for it is not rich, but the general land type includes the islands of Croil, Long Sault, Barnhart, and extends on the mainland southward to include the environs of Louisville, Madrid, Canton, and Potsdam. Somewhat more than 80 per cent of this loamy soil is devoted to farming, and well over 60 per cent is under cultivation. Not only the soil but the climate and the general location are particularly favorable for agricultural activity related to dairying. The area is very suitable for the raising of corn, oats, silage, small grains, hay, and the maintenance of pasture land.

As for the area inland from the St. Lawrence River, the agricultural value of the land is not very great. Much of the marginal lands, particularly in Jefferson County, have been turned back to forest in recent decades, and the reversion is facilitated by state legislation designed as conservation measures. Partly due to the marginal character of the land, and partly due to the encouraging forestry legislation, the shift from dairying or general agricultural activity to forest culture goes on, but at a decreasing rate.

In various parts of the country there are many areas, agricultural as to their general nature, wherein there is a tendency toward substantial conversion to forestry because of marginal or depleted land and soil. On such mar-

13

ginal areas often are scattered deserted farms and farm-houses. Many farmhouses in the reverted sections of the St. Lawrence area, however, are not abandoned. For the most part they have become unprofitable as farms, and even as forestry plantations, but the fact that they have been taken out of commercial farming does not preclude their mainte-nance as dwellings. The family automobile provides the non-commercial farm dweller with the means of transportation to nearby work places in industry and trade. Such rural fami-lies are quite commonly able to supplement their real in-come, and often their cash income, by maintaining a garden, at least of sufficient size to provide food for the family, and often a few odd farm animals — usually a cow or two.

Thus there is a fairly widespread reliance on part-time agriculture. This tends to invalidate attempts to deter-mine the standard of life in the area by use of a cash income index. Noncash income is obviously of some importance and perhaps of very great importance in a number of instances. The availability, use, and rather common reliance upon the family automobile is of considerable significance. There is in the St. Lawrence area approximately one automobile for each family in residence. Not only does the dependence on the auto emphasize rather dramatically the need for a more fully developed system of good roads in the area, but it also emphasizes a significant characteristic of the labor force. Labor has great spatial mobility, at least within the bound-aries of the general area we are discussing.

It becomes obvious that there has been consider-able decline in the agriculture of the St. Lawrence area and especially in Jefferson County over the past two or three decades. In spite of the decline the area is strikingly agri-cultural, especially for New York State. Eighteen per cent

14

of the entire labor force is engaged in agriculture. This is a high proportion for the state.

The St. Lawrence area poses some interesting comparisons in economic life. If we begin by excluding metropolitan New York City, it is clear that those who reside in the St. Lawrence tract live a kind of life that is more like that of the population of the entire country than of those who are residents of New York State. (See Table I.) Though many persons probably labor under the illusion that New York State, excluding the metropolitan area and its environs, is primarily an agricultural community, there were, in 1950, only slightly in excess of 6 per cent of the population engaged in agriculture. In the St. Lawrence area, however,

---

TABLE I

Livelihood Structure, 1950
Per Cent of Employed Persons in Selected Industry Groups

Industry Group	St. Lawrence Area	N.Y.S. Excl. Met. N.Y.	United States
Manufacturing	22.3	32.1	25.9
Agriculture	18.4	6.3	12.2
Wholesale and Retail Trade	17.1	18.2	18.8
Professional and Related Services	10.9	10.3	8.3
Business and Personal Services	9.2	8.4	8.7
Transportation, Communications, and Utilities	6.7	8.0	7.8
Forestry, Fishing, and Mining	1.9	.4	1.9
All Others	13.5	16.3	16.4

Source: United States Census.

---

there are more than 18 per cent so employed. A mere glance at the relevant statistics will lead one easily to the more valid characterization of "upper" New York State as distinctly an industrialized community, for nearly a third of its total working population was engaged in manufacturing, as of 1950. In the St. Lawrence area only 22 per cent were engaged in manufacturing categories. Thus the area, though somewhat typical of the United States as a whole, is atypical, in this respect, as a part of New York State.

A less dramatic discrepancy appears in the category of public utilities and transportation, wherein the St. Lawrence area employed less than 7 per cent of its working force, while about 8 per cent of the New York State working force is so occupied, again excluding metropolitan New York City. Should one apply the general rule that has been formulated from the American experience, i.e., that economic development implies industrialization, it becomes obvious that in 1950 the St. Lawrence area had not been developed as thoroughly as the rest of New York State outside the area of metropolitan New York.

Were one to include the metropolitan area of New York City in the comparison, so that the St. Lawrence area may be characterized relative to the entire state of New York, it is apparent that the agrarian, agricultural, nonmanufacturing nature of the area would be further emphasized, and perhaps more dramatically indicative of the lack of economic development in Jefferson, St. Lawrence, and Franklin Counties.

In spite of the fact that the area is less industrialized than the balance of the state, there has been a slight tendency toward industrialization. The pace of development, however, is a very slow one. The tendency is illustrated by the fact that, though in 1950, as was pointed out above, there were just a little more than 18 per cent of the population engaged in agriculture, two decades prior to that year almost a quarter of the residents were engaged in farming. Though in smaller proportion, the converse is true with regard to manufacturing, for in the year 1930 barely over 21 per cent of the labor force was engaged in manufacturing. By 1950, this figure had increased, slightly, to over 22 per cent.

In 1930 there were fewer persons in the labor force than in 1950, though the population rose during the twenty-year period from 220,288 to 229,248. Thus, in absolute figures, there were slightly fewer persons employed in manufacturing in 1950 than in 1930.

As one is likely to expect from the previous descriptions of the counties in the area, the relative concentrations of manufacturing employment differ rather widely from county to county within the St. Lawrence region. St. Lawrence County has the highest concentration with more than a quarter (25.9 per cent) of its employed persons working in industrial activity as of 1950. Franklin County is on the other extreme with only 17.6 per cent engaged in industry, while Jefferson County stands between the other two with 21.5 per cent of its working population employed in manufacturing.

Industry in America has usually tended toward location in or very near the large urban centers. Thus differences in the rates of manufacturing for several areas often represent the degrees of difference in urbanization. In the St. Lawrence area industry also tends to be located in or near the larger communities. St. Lawrence County, the most industrial of the three counties, contains the communities of Massena, Ogdensburg, Potsdam, Canton, Gouverneur,

17

and Heuvelton. Jefferson County has only two sizable communities, Carthage and Watertown. Watertown is the largest city of the whole area, however, and the county contains many small towns. Franklin County, at the other extreme, has only one major center at Malone. Tupper Lake, which is another center of population, does not lie in the area we have defined as the St. Lawrence, for it is located in the Adirondack State Park.

The St. Lawrence area has experienced an interesting pattern of industrial location. Watertown, Massena, and Ogdensburg are the three largest urban concentrations. As one would suspect, they account for a good share of the manufacturing employment. The concentration is even more distinct than that fact would imply, for, while more than 60 per cent of the total industrial manufacturing employment is within the *three* urban centers, one of them, Massena, dominates the other two. In fact, Massena dominates the whole area since it is the city in which is located the Aluminum Company of America plant. This one plant, engaged primarily in the manufacturing of pig and fabricated aluminum, employs more than 6,000 persons, which accounts for almost one-third of all the manufacturing employment of the entire area. The labor force at ALCOA is not all drawn from the immediate environs of Massena. There are some employees of the plant whose homes are located as far away as fifty miles.

In spite of the fact that manufacturing employment in the St. Lawrence area is concentrated in Massena, with lesser concentrations in the cities of Watertown and Ogdensburg, there were, in 1955, no less than 372 factories of one kind and another, with a grand total employment of about 20,000 persons.

Manufacturing employment in the St. Lawrence area, though not highly specialized as to skill, is for the most part concerned with the special industries engaged in the production of primary metals, paper and paper products, and machinery. Two-thirds of the entire manufacturing work force are employed in such industries. Watertown claims the second largest plant of the St. Lawrence area, for it is in this city that the New York Airbrake Company has located a plant that employs in the neighborhood of 2,200 people, a little more than a third the size of the force at ALCOA. The third most important employer of labor is concerned with the manufacture of paper and paper products. It is the St. Regis Paper Company, which is located near Carthage. It employs just under 1,000 persons.

Most of the remaining employers are small by comparison to the "Big Three." If, however, we can classify plants employing over one hundred persons as large, there are many such plants located throughout the larger population centers, that is, in Ogdensburg, Carthage, Gouverneur, Massena, and Malone. Further, there are many firms that employ just under one hundred persons. They are scattered through the area, but for the most part located in Newton Falls, Hailesboro, Brownville, Unionville, and Bombay. Thus, though there is a considerable concentration of industrial employment at Massena, there are employment centers elsewhere throughout the St. Lawrence area. But while the smaller plants dominate the area with respect to their number, the total employment in the small concerns is but a fraction of the employment in the large establishments. The pattern becomes clear when it is observed, for example, that only 9 per cent of the factories in the counties comprising the St. Lawrence tract employ over 80 per cent of the work-

19

ing force, while the smaller plants, constituting over 60 per cent of the number of manufacturing concerns, employ less than 1 per cent of the manufacturing employees.

Though the three largest communities in the area, Watertown (34,000), Ogdensburg (16,100), and Massena (13,100) account for more than a quarter (27 per cent) of the population, in 1950 almost half (46 per cent) of the people of the area lived in urban communities of 2,500 or more. But it is perhaps of some interest to note that Potsdam and Canton, two sizable communities for the area, are primarily devoted to the maintenance and serving of educational institutions. The State Teachers College and the Clarkson College of Technology, both in Potsdam, and St. Lawrence University and the New York State Agricultural and Technical Institute located in Canton represent important concentrations of people for the area. The population of both Potsdam and Canton is approximately 4,000, but neither is a very important manufacturing center. Well over 30 per cent of the total employment in Potsdam and over 25 per cent of the Canton employment is accounted for by the several educational institutions themselves. Nor is the population center at Ogdensburg wholly industrially oriented, for that city is the site of a large State Mental Hospital, a facility equipped to accommodate more than 2,000 patients, and employing a large staff. Further, it is important to note that a large military installation, Camp Drum, located just north of the community of Carthage, has employed as many as 15,000 persons during the summer season. Such communities tend to a very great degree to specialize in personal services rather than to emphasize manufacturing or mining. It should not be overlooked that the personal service type of employment is very important in the whole St. Lawrence area. This is particularly true, of course, in the summer season when the many summer resort establishments on Lake Ontario, and on the St. Lawrence River and its many smaller tributaries, are in full operation.

It is convenient for purposes of our analysis of the St. Lawrence area and its resources to establish standards by which communities may be classified. A reasonable classification may be made in terms of the services that are offered within a community. Our first classification may be that of a "primary community," which we shall define as any center, regardless of size, that supplies, in addition to the ordinary everyday goods and services, such specialized items and services as furniture, jewelry, household accessories, medical and dental care, legal advice, and other professional counsel. In other words, any community, which offers a broad spectrum of service to the consumer, may be referred to as a primary community.

We may arbitrarily define "secondary communities" as those having a minimum of ten retail stores and service units, though not necessarily covering a very wide gamut of such goods and services. However, in addition to groceries, taverns, and filling stations, which are found in each of the communities falling into this classification, they must have, to be a secondary community as we define it, at least four other retail businesses, e.g., auto sales rooms, implement, appliance, hardware, lumber, or livestock and feed stores. Such communities must also have at least two essential services such as a post office and auto repair establishment. Most of these secondary communities do indeed have the essential service of banking.

For our purposes the very smallest category may be that of the "tertiary community." Such communities may

21

be defined as those settlements which consist of at least five residential structures or other buildings used for commercial or cultural purposes, all the structures being located within a linear distance of a quarter of a mile. All tertiary communities have grocery stores, but they also may have, and usually do have, such establishments as taverns, filling stations, and auto repair shops.

Having established our standards we can now proceed to an appraisal of the St. Lawrence area on the basis of the size and nature of the communities it contains.

There are in all twelve primary communities in the area. Eight of them, Watertown, Ogdensburg, Massena, Malone, Potsdam, Gouverneur, Carthage, and Canton offer a rather complete gamut of goods and services, and each has a population in excess of 4,000 inhabitants. However, Clayton, Adams, Alexandria Bay, and Chateaugay all fall into the same category in that they offer a broad array of services, although their populations range only between 1,000 and 2,000.

All of the primary communities have matured administratively to the degree of having developed local agencies and techniques for administering such basic public services as those of water supply, refuse and garbage collection, sidewalk maintenance, water systems, sewer systems, public parks, docks, and cemeteries. Most of them, in addition to the above services, maintain separate fire protection systems, libraries, and even public nursing facilities. The county seats of all three counties represented in the St. Lawrence area can be considered as central trading areas, and each of them is thus included among the twelve primary communities. Watertown, in addition to being the largest population center, is the richest community in terms of the

22

number and variety of services offered.

There are twenty-eight communities in the St. Lawrence area that fall within our classification of "secondary." More than half of them have either a central or district high school. A total of seventeen of the twenty-eight are incorporated under New York State law. Communities in this category, of course, are lacking many of the basic needs of fully developed centers, but their greatest deficiency appears in the various personal and professional services. Generally the secondary communities have practicing physicians, but they often lack adequate dental services, and their recreation facilities are deficient or unsatisfactory. Many of the secondary communities are without a motion picture theater, but most of them contain dance halls, restaurants, taverns, and bowling alleys. It is interesting that a number of the secondary communities maintain important industrial components, which are in some instances as important as the industrial components of the primary communities.

Ninety-seven tertiary communities are contained in the area. Seventeen are in Franklin County, and forty each in Jefferson and St. Lawrence Counties. Often such communities have a school of some kind, a post office, and a church or some other community organization. But in general they contain little else by way of community facilities.

The pattern of dispersal of the three kinds of communities is varied. The larger or primary centers of the area tend to be spaced from thirty to fifty miles apart. The secondary communities are generally about ten miles apart, although in some instances they are as near to each other as five miles. The large number of tertiary communities really reflect no apparent pattern of location except that they are for the most part situated in the farming areas. Only a very few of these smallest communities lie on a railroad, but all of them are located on reasonably good highways.

The St. Lawrence area is served by three railroad routes. The Syracuse-Watertown-Massena line of the New York Central connects with the Canadian National and thus serves as an entry and exit to the north and south. There is also a New York Central line running east of the area from Utica through Malone to Montreal. Further, the Rutland Railroad running from Ogdensburg serves a number of communities en route to Malone, and then to Rouses Point. None of these railroads carry much in the way of passenger traffic, however, since in the entire St. Lawrence area public highways are the more important travel routes.

It is interesting to note at this point that in our discussion of the nature and location of the various communities lying within the St. Lawrence area there has been little or no mention of the St. Lawrence River itself. Any discussion of this sort tends, indeed, to illuminate a most significant fact: the St. Lawrence River is relatively unimportant to the area. The river and its shore line, of course, furnish important recreation areas, but in general the communities which we have been discussing tend to turn their backs on the river and to look more to the hinterlands. For example, of the seven population centers located on or near the river, there are only two which are large enough to rank as genuine urban settlements. They are Ogdensburg and Massena. Yet Massena is not really located on the river, and Ogdensburg indicates little if any dependence upon the river. Dairying, industry, and tourism are the general economic supports of the area, rather than the river.

Thus it becomes clear that such a development as the St. Lawrence Seaway may radically change the economic and social nature of the whole area. If it is to contribute anything to economic development there, it will be a wholly new and extensively effective resource. The river may well become the main highway to bring in raw materials and to take out finished products, or it is equally possible that the river shore line may become sites for warehousing and trans-shipping activities. At any rate, whatever the particular use of the river comes to be, it is almost certain to provide new and expanding elements in what has been and is now a relatively stable economic structure.

THE HUMAN COMMUNITY

Perhaps one of the most significant social and economic facts about the St. Lawrence region is that each of the more important settled and developed communities is for the most part the center of its own economic hinterland. There is little economic and social overlap throughout the whole area. Each of these communities, though not self-sufficient, has only a moderate degree of industrial dependence upon neighboring communities. Each center is connected more or less directly with the great markets of the United States or Canada. Watertown is the center of the closely settled Ontario Hills on the northern border of the Tughill country. Gouverneur, located in the midst of the western Adirondacks, serves somewhat as the center of a mining area. The twin cities of Canton and Potsdam dominate the rich dairy lands of the St. Lawrence Hills. Ogdensburg and Massena reign over the productive St. Lawrence Plain. Malone commands the gateway to the northern Adirondacks, while Carthage oversees the entrance to the Black River Country with its

27

paper industry and mineral activity.

Yet in viewing the economic activity of the area one should by no means overlook the human resources which are not contained in the larger centers. About 100,000 people live in the smaller communities and in rural areas, although, as has been pointed out, all of the rural inhabitants are not necessarily engaged in farming.

The most important city in the whole area, in terms of retail and wholesale trade, is Watertown. It contains only about 15 per cent of the total population, yet this city does more than a third of the retail business, which is a commanding figure in spite of the fact that some of the sales derive from Lewis and Oswego Counties. The larger communities, then, account for most of the general trading of the St. Lawrence area. Such centers of trade are made possible through the existence of a fairly adequate, though not fully developed, road system and the omnipresence of the automobile. Although the population of the area is scattered over a wide expanse, most of the retail purchases, except for such convenience items as groceries and other foodstuffs, are made in a relatively few of the larger, primary communities. The centering of retail trade in this manner provides a kind of cohesiveness and even establishes a basis for community spirit in many of the larger centers.

There are many communities of appreciable size, by the standards of the sparsely settled St. Lawrence area, but, other than Watertown, they are very small by the more common metropolitan standards. Small urban concentrations such as these cannot very often afford to provide the many and extraordinary services or public works either for the residents of the communities, or for whatever industry is located within their environs. Nor are the three county governments contained in the St. Lawrence tract wealthy enough to afford very large expenditures for such purposes. About all that can be done, in spite of whatever desire and pride that may exist in these small communities, is to supply the bare necessary amenities and services more or less typical of modern small-town life.

But such financial inabilities to provide the ideal in community services pose a psychological dilemma in the minds of community-conscious people in the area. Because of the many deficiencies in community services, self-reliance tends to be maximized in the larger communities. But self-reliance on the part of the individual contributes to community pride and determination to meet the growing demands of modern life. Business, trade, and social organizations of many types are of great importance and exist in numbers throughout both the urban and rural sections of the St. Lawrence country. Ironically enough, though extreme local self-reliance tends to force solutions to public problems and tailor them to the resources at hand, the solutions arrived at very often suffer from the lack of broad vision and integration. It is painfully obvious, for example, that not every town on the river can become an important river port. But public-spirited citizens in virtually every town which has an easy access to the St. Lawrence River have at some time devoted much of their energy to the building up of their own and public hopes toward making their community a full-fledged river port.

Pride in such instances has indeed often gone before a fall, and the inevitable let-down is very hard on public morale. Perhaps the root of the problem is that most of the communities in question are engaged in a feverish competition for economic advancement. But aspirations for such

29

advancement must be based much more upon the facts of economic life than upon local pride, for when it is based primarily on the latter, what begins as something rare and admirable turns out to be wasted.

There is at least one community in the area that is aroused to civic consciousness with a good deal of self-righteousness. The village of Massena, with its population slightly in excess of 14,000 has been, since the beginning of the construction projects, the focus of a great amount of new economic activity. But the construction activity is, of course, almost wholly temporary. Most of the work that is centered in or near Massena will in a few years be reduced drastically, and by 1958 the employment of construction labor engaged in building the Barnhart Island project should be virtually nil. There is always the possibility that unexpected changes to preclude such reduction will take place in the planning and development. But this is not apparent at the moment.

Barnhart Island is the site of the Power Project, and lies wholly within the town of Massena though about five miles from the center of the village of Massena. The Long Sault Seaway Canal will pass just within two miles of the village. Further, it has been estimated that more than two-thirds, possibly as much as 70 per cent, of the navigation and power work, which will be required for the Seaway and Power Projects on the American side of the St. Lawrence River, will be consummated very near to the village of Massena. This little community is thus faced with immense construction problems and accelerated general economic activities that are quite unique in the St. Lawrence area. As many as 9,000 workers of one kind and another will have been employed in and near the village of Massena by 1958.

As one would expect, a community located on the focal point of the two great projects will experience a rapid growth in the scope and amount of administrative and social problems. Massena is experiencing such a radical and sudden increase in importance as an employment and construction center that it is bound to have great difficulty, at the very best, in meeting the demands put upon it to furnish such basic services as housing, schooling, sewage disposal, parking facilities, roads and bridges, water supply, and recreation. And the strain has not been much less for the fact that the residents of the village have long anticipated such a boom. Citizens of the community had been conscious for some time of the fact that they lived in the center of one of the best remaining undeveloped hydroelectric power sites in North America, and even though they were thus psychologically prepared for its ultimate fruition, they could not possibly have prepared for the physical influx that would almost double their population in a few years time. The citizens of Massena have almost wholly to rely upon their own ingenuity in suffering the impact, for while there have been many projects of comparable size in other communities, seldom have they caused so direct and sudden an effect upon such a community as Massena. The usual pattern has been the establishment of a brand new population center along with a construction project.

The political and social problems of the community of Massena have been a source of awe to most local groups and individual citizens. Efforts to meet the problem of housing, for example, were for the most part so unsuccessfully handled by local agents that outside concerns, with perhaps little interest in the organization and beauty of the community, moved in to take financial advantage of the boom.

Local inflation has begun to loom as a real problem. The tax structure will have to change if the local community is to finance improvements and services, yet the resistance to such change is typical even in Massena. While the size of school populations are creating a classroom and teacher shortage problem in almost every community in the United States, few towns in the country are confronted with the strained situation facing Massena. Problems such as these lead to intensely difficult relations between locally responsible officials and those of outside agencies participating in the development of the Seaway and Power Projects. Frustrations are often released in sharp comments on the part of both.

There have been many attempts on the part of local officials, private consultants, and state agencies to plan for the development of the community in a more or less orderly fashion. Most of the plans have been abandoned as unrealistic or lacking in thoroughness. The lack of progress in solving programing problems has not led to harmonious feelings. Local authorities have blamed state and other officials and agencies for the confusion. State officials have blamed local lack of vision and patience, and, in the meantime, whatever genuine "community spirit" there existed in the Massena area has been in danger of rapid deterioration. A clear illustration is an incident of lack of cooperation between local and state officials early in 1955, in which Mr. Floyd Hosmer, a Supervisor from the town of Massena, criticized the Power Authority in a public letter as follows:

For the life of me, I have been unable to understand some of the poorly planned and seemingly asinine policies promoted [by the Authority] *in this project. They have moved into this area to build approximately a three or four million dollar development, without any advance preparation or plans for access to roads, streets, bridges, railroads, housing, school or hospital facilities or even proper office facilities for their engineering and other staffs, which to date had [sic] withstood two fire losses with attendant loss of valued records and work. Our roads and bridges have been used and destroyed with abandon, even totally, in some sections, and the lives of our residents have been needlessly placed in jeopardy and danger, as well as their property with very little consideration shown them under these same policies. . . .*

You have my word in this matter, that if nothing is done to relieve this situation in the weeks immediately ahead and it appears that another emergency may arise in this connection, I shall not hesitate to ask Governor Harriman to use his power and authority in declaring this an emergency area and to stop all project construction until conditions have been alleviated. . . .[1]

The letter partly quoted above may well have been an expression of the sentiment of the community. Though it was not addressed to him, the criticism was immediately answered by Mr. Robert Moses, the Chairman of the Power Authority, as follows:

We have a copy of your letter. . . . This Authority does not have the slightest interest in your local political shenanigans, aspirations and personalities in St. Lawrence County. . . .

---

[1]**Massena Observer**, May 12, 1955.

The Authority has issued statements on policy from time to time and these have been put in language understandable to all. We have not made rash promises to relieve the local area of all its normal responsibilities. This project will bring great benefits to the St. Lawrence area and particularly to the town of Massena. . . .

You will find, if you will keep your shirt on and file your tongue, that we are using sufficient initiative and resourcefulness to attract substantial industries to this area.

. . . Your letter is just cheap local politics.

We are anxious to deal with responsible elected and other representatives. Our previous conferences and conversations with you led us to believe you were in this category. We shall continue to follow this procedure, in spite of some disappointment.[1]

Perhaps the reader may feel that several tongues needed filing on this occasion and may further agree that Mr. Moses spoke from a more sagacious mood when he pointed out earlier that "No large undertaking can be built without dislocation and other community problems. In this instance, the seriousness of the impact will depend to a great extent upon the willingness of the community to accept temporary inconvenience and to cooperate in the face of some hardships, anticipating an era of expansion and prosperity along the St. Lawrence."[2]

There is some danger that the "temporary inconvenience" will do permanent damage to the spirits of the

[1]Syracuse Post-Standard, May 13, 1955.

[2]New York Power Authority, **St. Lawrence Power**, August 10, 1954, page 4.

local residents. But that does not necessarily have to happen. There will certainly be countless readjustments necessary on the part of individuals and institutions. It may well be that Massena will double its size, or at least be transformed from a small town to a bustling city. But such rapid urbanization as is indicated for Massena has always resulted in radical alterations in the structure and function of community life. The people of Massena, or any of the other communities in the area, should not give up on local problems simply because they are difficult, and it is indeed certain that local and state political energies should not work against each other, but should try to proceed harmoniously.

Not only Massena, but the whole underdeveloped St. Lawrence area must rely on the public administrative bodies of the state and federal governments. This is obviously an economic necessity. Roads, assistance in education, and planning are among the services that would not at all be properly developed without considerable help from outside the immediate area. The fact of the federal government's undertaking of the Seaway Project in cooperation with the Canadian national government and the fact of New York State's construction of the Power Project in cooperation with the provincial government of Ontario underline and dramatize the tremendously important roles which outside public agencies are to play in the development of the St. Lawrence area.

The New York State Power Authority, for example, is the administrative authority that has been charged with the responsibility for the operation of the Power Project. In spite of the fact that it is a state agency, it is required by law to secure its funds from the private capital market. The authority has sold bonds worth a total of $350,000,000 which have been purchased by bond houses throughout the continental United States.

Contracts between prospective users of power and the Power Authority, that at this writing have already been approved by either the Governor or the Authority, will account for the consumption of the American share of the power output. They further indicate the intention on the part of both the Reynolds Metals Company and General Motors to build new plants in the Massena area. But in order to avoid too severe a disruption in the economic process around Massena, the Reynolds Company has planned not to build its plant until the work on the Seaway and Power Project begins to taper off. Similarly the work on the General Motors plant will not begin until some time after the peak of construction employment has been reached.

It is clear, then, that there will be a rather sustained building boom in Massena. The present high level of employment will be extended in time and the crowded living conditions will continue. This means, of course, that when the production work gets fully under way, the whole pattern of the resources of Massena and the area around Massena will have to be expanded to meet all the day-to-day needs of the rising population and the rising standard of living in the community. The prospects of a continued building program have already triggered prolific community activity for dealing with the public problems that generally accompany sudden growth. However, it becomes ever clearer that the community resources will be strained beyond capacity unless they are buttressed by outside financial and administrative assistance.

From the gigantic construction projects down to the provision of most of the community services, there will be several levels of government coming together in Massena. Although the brunt of the initial impact is being borne by this little village, the same process, in varying degrees of intensity, will be repeated in other parts of the St. Lawrence area. One might well hope, however, that as the massive power of state and national governments moves in to affect Massena and other communities of the area, that the primary human relationships that have been traditionally so important to the operation of democracy in America will be enhanced and enriched and not stifled or destroyed.

Long ago Thomas Jefferson warned us that "when we get piled upon one another in cities . . . we shall become corrupt as in Europe, and go eating one another as they do there." Jefferson's prediction may not come true for the communities of the St. Lawrence area, but his insight is still important to bear in mind since all too often small towns and villages in America have become cities, only to lose their character as genuine human communities. Some lonesome people in this complex impersonal world go their separate ways and never find the full satisfaction of comradeship and lasting human association without which life is an intolerable, solitary process. Patience and a cooperative spirit, however, can help to preserve those associations which seem necessary to purposefulness in life and to a healthy democratic society.

POPULATION, INCOME, AND INDUSTRIAL STRUCTURE

There is not much that government does or can do about population growth. Estimates of the increase in population of New York State during the first half of the present decade tend to show a steady rise in the number of people living in the state. The New York State Department of Health estimates indicate that the population of the state increased by about 7.5 per cent between 1950 and 1955. During the same years the population also rose in the St. Lawrence area, but at a slower rate. The increase in St. Lawrence County was 5.5 per cent, Jefferson County a bare 3 per cent, and in Franklin County only 2.5 per cent. Only Massena in the entire St. Lawrence area showed a ratio of increase in excess of that for the population of New York State. Here the rise was a mere 10 per cent in spite of the fact that some migration of construction personnel to that center had begun early in 1954.

A close look at the population distribution of the area is very revealing and instructive to any who are appraising its resources. (Table II.) In the year 1950 over 22 per cent of the population were less than fourteen years of age while just under 19 per cent were over the age of fifty-five. The counties in the St. Lawrence area, however, present a rather different pattern. In Franklin County, there were over 28 per cent who were younger than fourteen years and nearly 20 per cent over fifty-five years of age; and there was but very insignificant difference in these relations in Jefferson and St. Lawrence Counties. Thus the whole St. Lawrence area, in 1950, had a considerably larger proportion of its population *under* fourteen years of age and *over* fifty-five years of age than was true of New York State generally. The urban centers within the area are much nearer the general pattern of the state than the St. Lawrence area as a whole. Further, slightly more than 45 per cent of the population of

TABLE II

Distribution of Population by Age, 1950 (Per Cent)

	Under 5	5-14 Years	15-24 Years	25-44 Years	45-54 Years	55-64 Years	65 Years and Over
New York State	9.2	13.4	13.4	31.7	13.6	10.2	8.5
Franklin County	11.2	17.6	14.4	26.3	11.6	9.2	9.8
Jefferson County	10.8	16.4	12.8	26.4	11.8	10.0	11.8
Watertown	10.2	14.3	12.9	27.8	12.5	10.3	11.9
St. Lawrence Co.	11.4	17.4	16.1	25.9	10.5	8.7	10.1
Massena	12.6	17.6	14.7	31.1	11.3	7.3	5.3
Ogdensburg	9.5	14.7	12.6	26.0	12.3	10.5	14.4

Source: New York State Department of Commerce, **New York State Business Facts, Northern Area, 1954 Supplement,** p. 3.

New York State fell within the twenty-five- to fifty-five-year age bracket, while the St. Lawrence area counties have only from 36 to 38 per cent in this particular age group. These statistics are very meaningful and significant for they indicate an important and unique characteristic of the area, i.e., the proportion of people in their most productive years is much smaller in the area than in the state of New York as a whole.

One can only speculate as to reasons for the unusual population distribution by age, but what appears to have happened is that many persons in their late teens or early twenties have sought and apparently found jobs outside the area. Many of them in this generation have undoubtedly moved to the larger, principal population concentrations in the area itself, but there are many others who have probably gone to Rochester, Syracuse, Utica, or Schenectady, and perhaps to other large cities of the state and the United States to earn their living and make their way.

Such a phenomenon in population movement is not unusual in America, yet the degree in which it has taken place in the St. Lawrence area is extraordinary. From the viewpoint of those young people involved, the movement is certainly understandable. From the more general viewpoint of the well-being of the local economy and society, however, it might very well be disastrous. Migrations of this kind always tend to detract from the community's strength in that they draw off the better educated, more active, more imaginative, and more productive people. Migration, in a sense, really amounts to an export of capital from what is already a capital-poor area. No public administrator and certainly no parent need be reminded that to feed, clothe, educate, and care for young people is an extremely expensive proposition, and it should thus be clear that to train and bring up the young people of any community is to accumulate capital within it. When such young people leave the area, they take to their new home, wherever they may be, an investment of many thousands of dollars and many hours of both public and private nurture and care. Yet the trend toward migration of young people from the area, which is in truth nothing short of capital export, can neither be stopped nor reversed until much richer social and economic opportunities for a full and good life are provided. Were the young folk induced to stay, because of the new resources and potential of the area, the St. Lawrence country would be richer by the people it retained as well as the cost of rearing them.

Turning to another economic category, that of income, we find the United States census studies helpful, for in 1950 the Census secured certain information regarding median incomes on a county basis. Median income figures are not as fully informative as one might wish them to be, but they are useful for comparisons. Median income only measures the income of families falling exactly in the middle of a ranking of family incomes from low to high. Thus half of the families in any particular county have incomes of less than the median, while half have incomes higher than the median. In 1950 the median income for the United States was $3,073. In the same year it was $3,487 per family in New York State. Franklin County, which is more agricultural than the other two counties in the St. Lawrence area, had a median income per family of $2,474—more than $1,000 less than that of the state as a whole. Jefferson and St. Lawrence Counties were somewhat higher than Franklin County, $2,859 and $2,769 respectively, but still behind both the national and state medians. As has been pointed out earlier, these statistics must be interpreted with caution because they do not take into consideration "income in kind" or any other noncash income. The total amounts of such income may be rather significant in the St. Lawrence counties, yet it is doubted that taking them into account would *radically* alter the general picture. Thus, even though we do not include the "income" efforts on the part of many families in the area by way of garden plots, family cows, etc., it is nevertheless apparent that in 1950 the median income for the St. Lawrence area was somewhat below the median income for New York State as a whole. In all probability this relationship has not changed appreciably since 1950.

There are further radical discrepancies within the area itself, for personal income payments, in 1952, though only slightly higher in St. Lawrence County than in Jefferson, in the former county they were almost three times that of Franklin County. (Table III.) The per capita income in 1950, however, was $1,000 in Franklin County, $1,310 in Jefferson County, and $1,156 in St. Lawrence County.

As to housing in the St. Lawrence area, a comparison with the state as a whole again puts the area in an unfavorable light. On the average the residents of the area live in pre-World War I homes, but more than 60 per cent of them own their homes. In the state as a whole, less than 40 per cent own their homes, but a far greater proportion of people outside the St. Lawrence area tend to live in houses that were built after 1913 than within the area. However, one should not assume that homes in the St. Lawrence area are antiquated or primitive in any sense. More than half of them have indoor toilets and baths with hot and cold running water. More than half of them have modern central heating plants, and many more than three-quarters of them have mechanical refrigeration. Data such as these, furthermore, are county data, and it should be remembered that they include homes in the most rural areas as well as the homes in the centers of population. It can probably be assumed with safety that the urban homes are equipped with more modern facilities, on the average, than rural homes.

There are other important indications of the level of living in the St. Lawrence country. Of considerable significance, for example, is the number of private passenger cars the people of the area have had at their disposal. During the year 1952 there were 11,673 registrations of passenger cars in Franklin County, 24,740 in Jefferson County, and 25,779 in St. Lawrence County. Thus there was one such automobile for approximately every three and one-half persons in the whole St. Lawrence area. Such a proportion of privately owned transportation per capita is a remarkably

TABLE III

Personal Income Payments to Individuals
in the St. Lawrence Area 1952

	Franklin Co.	Jefferson Co.	St. Lawrence Co.
Total Personal Income Payments	$46,700,000	$114,500,000	$120,100,000
Wages and Salaries	64.0%	67.0%	71.0%
Proprietors Income	18.2%	14.9%	13.3%
Property Income	9.2%	10.2%	8.1%
Other	0.0%	0.0%	0.0%

Source: New York Department of Commerce.

44

high one and means that there is approximately one private passenger auto for each family, on the average. Automobiles or some other personally owned means of transportation, are a virtual necessity in any section in which the population is so dispersed as that of the St. Lawrence country, and one would expect a rather high ratio of ownership. Nevertheless, such indicators as the existence of the great number of automobiles and the evident nonmoney real income secured by a high proportion of the resident families, make it fairly clear that the standard of life of the average family in the North Country, while not extremely high, is certainly far above any subsistence level, and that it probably embraces many luxuries as well as necessities.

The St. Lawrence area has developed a unique pattern of employment skewed radically toward three main industries which employ almost two-thirds of the labor complement in manufacturing. The three industries are paper and paper products, primary metals, and machinery. Thirty-one per cent of the employment in the area is in primary metals, 19 per cent in paper and paper products, and 15 per cent in machinery products. Taken together, however, the three main industries constitute only 10 per cent of the total number of manufacturing establishments.

Of the total of 372 plants in the area, one-third are engaged in working on lumber and wood products. But this large number of establishments employs a bare 5 per cent of the total manufacturing employment. Likewise, while only 7 per cent of the total manufacturing employment is engaged in the processing of food, they are very small establishments, and there are over one hundred such plants in spite of the fact that they account for but a small proportion of all labor engaged in manufacturing. These small plants

45

are scattered over the whole North Country, though slightly concentrated in and around Watertown and Adams. There are other industries such as printing, publishing, apparel, chemical and allied products, but each of these employs only a scattering of people.

As of 1956, almost half of the 372 establishments in the St. Lawrence area, located principally in Ogdensburg, Massena, and Watertown (but many of them also in other urban centers), worked on various materials which had been processed or semifabricated in other factories. Thus these various firms, which account for nearly 80 per cent of the manufacturing employment in the area, are almost wholly dependent on other firms, located for the most part outside the area itself, for their supplies of processed materials for further manufacture. There are some notable exceptions to this generalization. The main exception is the lumber industry, accounting for one-third of the establishments, though employing only 12 per cent of the employees. These plants obtain their materials directly from the local forests. Pulp plants and saw mills, all working on raw resources, are typically located in the very small communities and obtain their materials from directly adjacent areas. There are, further, another 6 per cent of the employees of the area engaged in processing of agricultural products. Such firms account for about 16 per cent of the establishments in the area and are, by and large, processing milk that is secured from the local milk shed.

About 3 per cent of the factories in the area, accounting for approximately the same proportion of the manufacturing employment, engage in the processing of mineral materials. Their greatest concentration is near and in Gouverneur, which is the center of the talc products industry in the North Country. There is, furthermore, some stonecutting at Redwood and Burke. Virtually every primary population concentration in the St. Lawrence area has one or more establishments performing some work with concrete and concrete products, largely for the local building industry.

Most of the factory employment in the St. Lawrence area, however, — that of the primary metals, paper and paper products, and machinery industries — rely for their raw materials on other concerns. Thus the St. Lawrence country is not an area that is important in the production of raw materials. This conclusion is both corroborated and borne out by other indications. For example, nearly two-thirds of the manufacturing employees work in establishments that secure the bulk of their materials from the national market-at-large as distinct from the local market, although this fact is relevant to only about a quarter of the total number of plants in the area. Factories in this category are located in every large community in the St. Lawrence area, most especially in the vicinities of Watertown, Massena, Malone, and Ogdensburg.

On the other hand, less than 15 per cent of the manufacturing labor force work in factories that secure all or most of their raw materials locally. Just over half the number of plants fall in this category. Even the whole region of New York State is of secondary importance as a supplier of raw materials to the factories and plants of the St. Lawrence area. There are only 16 per cent of the plants, which employ but 6 per cent of the manufacturing labor force, that are oriented to New York State for material supply. It is interesting to note that about 8 per cent of the establishments, employing 20 per cent of the factory labor, received their raw materials from neither the local nor the state, nor the national market, but from "other" sources outside (largely Canadian) the United States. Among such plants are paper mills, moccasin factories, newspapers, metal plants, and chemical plants located in Carthage, Malone, Potsdam, Gouverneur, Ogdensburg, and Deferiet.

The indication is unmistakable, then, that even though the St. Lawrence area is geographically located on the very periphery of the central United States-Canadian manufacturing axis, the area is actually a part of the United States national market when it comes to buying the materials for industrial production.

As the St. Lawrence area is not important in terms of supplying its own raw materials, neither is it important as a market for the sale of locally manufactured products. Over 20 per cent of the factories in the region, employing more than 80 per cent of the factory labor force, produced goods sold in the nation-wide market. All of the large plants and most of the medium sized establishments fall into this category. Conversely, less than one-tenth of the total manufacturing employment, though representative of 62 per cent of the factories, produced for local markets. From these data it is obvious that all of these plants are small ones. They are typically such types of concerns as saw mills, dairies, bakeries, or bottling works. The market area which comprises the whole of New York State, as distinct from the local St. Lawrence area market, consumes the production of only 8 per cent of the manufacturing employment, though this figure accounts for approximately 15 per cent of the total number of plants. The concerns which lie in this category are mainly the food, apparel, and paper factories of Jefferson and St. Lawrence Counties.

This discussion leads to a significant conclusion

48

regarding the nature of the economy of the St. Lawrence area. Both the data concerning the market served by St. Lawrence manufactories and those concerning the sources of materials secured by the factories in the area carry one to substantially the same judgment. The St. Lawrence area is not a "primitive" closed, self-sufficient economy. It is a segment of the whole industrial complex of the United States. Manufacturing industry in the North Country buys its raw materials in the general market, mainly of the United States, and it is likewise mainly concerned with selling in the general United States market.

The status of economic development as often depends upon a state of mind as upon actual economic resources. In 1956, as an attempt to determine the nature of opinion on the part of industrial management in the area, a questionnaire was addressed to all the known manufacturers in the St. Lawrence country. Forty-two per cent, or 154 factories, responded in the survey. Such a high response perhaps indicates a rather marked interest on the part of business concerns in local economic circumstances.

Of the responding firms, 89 per cent indicated their feeling that labor conditions were the most important factor in their own decision to locate in the St. Lawrence area, and the overwhelming majority, 86 per cent of the respondents, considered labor as currently a favorable or advantageous factor in factory location in the North Country. Labor stability, the general status of labor relations, and the over-all willingness and cooperativeness of labor were all reported as very important considerations, while only nineteen of the total number of respondents considered labor conditions as unfavorable in any fashion.

As to the markets, 62 per cent of the 154 respond-

49

ents in the survey viewed the local market position as an important consideration in their location, while most of these establishments looked upon their particular geographic location as favorable to their own marketing programs. On the whole, local markets were considered very good, since only twenty firms considered market conditions as unfavorable. However, all twenty sold to both national and local markets, and the complaint was that since the St. Lawrence area is somewhat off the beaten track, firms catering to national markets find themselves in a somewhat unfavorable competitive position as compared to other large nation-wide firms.

The availability of raw materials is generally an important consideration in industrial location. Eighty-six establishments, comprising 56 per cent of the respondents, viewed the easy availability of materials for their operation as an important consideration in their location. As many as 81 per cent of the respondents thought that their location in this respect was a favorable one regardless of the weight given to that consideration at the time of location. This is a rather illuminating and interesting response, since it will be remembered that nearly nine-tenths of all industry in the area, as measured by the number of persons employed, secures its raw materials from *outside* the St. Lawrence area. The illuminating quality of the response is that it tends to indicate that the existing transportation network is largely satisfactory, at least for the industry now located in the area.

As one might well expect, taxes were reported by the manufacturers in the area as an important factor in locating industrial establishments. Eighty-three concerns, or 54 per cent of the respondents, viewed taxes as generally important, yet, interestingly enough in a tax-conscious world, two-thirds of the respondents considered the present tax structure in the area favorable. The remainder of the firms responding considered the factor of taxes as being of no very great significance, except that a small minority of them stated that local taxes in a few of the larger communities were a little high.

The existence of power in the area is not extremely significant to the present industrial structure, for only a third of the reporting factories considered it important, and an overwhelming majority, 80 per cent, considered the power factor favorable in the area. The main private supplier of power in the St. Lawrence area is the Niagara Mohawk Power Corporation, which maintains a good reputation with its industrial customers. The cost of power, its adequacy of supply, its reliability, propriety as to type, and general service facilities were all considered important by the respondents. It should be noted, however, that the great bulk of industry now existing in the St. Lawrence country is not distinctly power-oriented. The Aluminum Company of America and the St. Regis Paper Company are, of course, the two most major exceptions. The Reynolds Metals Company will fall into this category when it is in production.

One of the most crucial questions for the future of the area is that of the effect that the new power resource from the Barnhart Island Project will have on the manufacturing and industrial profile of the St. Lawrence. Obviously the presence of the Power Project may radically change the status of the power factor as a consideration in industrial location.

In view of our earlier comments concerning the apocryphal legends about the climate, it is not surprising that only 10 per cent of the St. Lawrence area manufacturers considered the climate important enough to remark upon in their responses to the questionnaire. Based upon 65 degrees Fahrenheit, only the northern, colder part has 8,000 to 9,000 annual degree-days, as contrasted with 6,000 to 7,000 annual degree-days for the greater portion of the manufacturing belt of the area. Heating costs are, of necessity, relatively high. Though such costs do not compare favorably with heating costs in the warmer climates, they are not commonly felt to be a deterrent since they are apparently more than offset by temperate summer conditions that are much more conducive to high production than in communities farther south.

As a general conclusion, it may be said that the St. Lawrence area, with its few large industrial firms and its many small establishments, has an over-all industrial complement that has certainly adjusted well to the many advantages and disadvantages of the area. In fact, the whole area had definitely achieved, prior to the development of a specific program for the construction of a Seaway and Power Project, a certain industrial stability. Such stability is unique in the dynamic American society. But the St. Lawrence area, in so far as its economic activity is concerned, has not been especially dynamic. The American economy, the adjacent New York State economy, and the Canadian manufacturing economy have all grown at a faster rate than that of the St. Lawrence area.

THE ST. LAWRENCE AREA
IN PERSPECTIVE

As we have discovered, the St. Lawrence area had become by the early 1950's a rather stable economy and, more than that, we have seen that it has been less well developed than other parts of New York and the nation. Yet in most other respects the economy of the area is similar to that of adjacent parts of the national scene since it is very definitely a segment of the national economy. The American economy is characterized by the fact that the general forces of the market tend to determine the geographical location of industry and manufacturing. In a free enterprise system, where each may make his own decisions and suffer from his own mistakes or benefit from his own good judgment, advantages of location are carefully weighed by the entrepreneur. For this reason, it is probably safe to assume that the whole St. Lawrence area economic stature represents an achievement of about the maximum that the pre-1954 economic forces would produce or permit. Stated more directly and simply, the assumption is that up to the time of the consideration

53

of the St. Lawrence Seaway and the Barnhart Island Power Project, business, industry, and agriculture were developed to the point where they were using the resources of the St. Lawrence area that technology had already tapped, or that political policy had already made possible, about as effectively as they could be used in any free market economy.

Then, in 1954, something new was added in the way of reachable resources. Almost immediately various appraisals of the economic potential of the St. Lawrence area by those who live there, and even by others who were concerned about the matter, underwent drastic and radical changes. The first burst of enthusiasm led, as might well have been expected, to feelings that the Seaway and the Power Project were going to make fabulous and drastic changes in the area so as to convert it into a kind of "wonderland," or that it would be transformed into a place that might be described as "St. Lawrence Unlimited." Every genuine expectation was enhanced and magnified by wishful thinking. But such hopes and fancies were soon found to have little basis in reality.

Before long, an almost inevitable reaction had set in, and it became more fashionable to speak of the future of the area in somewhat derisive terms. Some even predicted that the people in the St. Lawrence country would merely sit on the river bank and watch the bigger and better ships go *past*, that there was to be a great power source, but that it would either be exported from the area itself or, if it remained, would not create many new jobs for the people living in the vicinity. Cynical and unjustified low expectations almost wholly replaced their opposite extreme.

By 1956, however, a much more balanced and certainly more reasonable set of expectations began to emerge in the minds of both the people of the area and those outsiders who took an interest in the possibilities for development there. Realistic and thus more valid appraisals are beginning to replace the vague and hopeful whims and the later disillusionment.

The truth is that while this very process of heating and cooling of spirits has been going on, the two new and very important resources have already begun to change the economic complexion of the St. Lawrence country. It is very likely that the two new projects, the Seaway and the Power Project, will prove to be both direct causes and catalytic agents for some significant business, industrial, and agricultural changes. Analysts should know better, but many too often overlook the frequently significant economic consequences of relatively small changes in business activity and public attitudes toward business. As the American experience has shown over and over again, business "climate" and the general business attitudes of a community can spell the difference between success and failure of individual firms, especially those firms which are established to provide goods and services to residents of the area in question.

In the context of the above, a crucial question is posed. Will the St. Lawrence Seaway, as a great transportation facility, and the Barnhart Island Power Project carry with them sufficient economic potential and instill sufficient business enthusiasm and spirit for economic development, so as to alter importantly the previous economic profile of the St. Lawrence area?

Although this is surely the most important question raised for the future of the region, there is really no very definite answer that can be given. One of the greatest variables in the situation, and one which makes it impossible

55

to predict with any great degree of accuracy, is the speed, the depth, and general nature of the reaction of businessmen and investors. Further, it is difficult to tell in advance whether the advantages in economic potential of the St. Lawrence area, when developed, will actually make it economically superior to other areas of the country at any particular future date. It must be remembered that the St. Lawrence is not the only place in the country that is to undergo significant changes. All over the United States certainly, and in many parts of Canada, there are areas which, though they have been as stable economically as the St. Lawrence area of New York State, have recently become dynamic and are beginning to come up to their potential because of some significant resource changes. It is nonetheless true that businessmen and investors must make up their minds on the basis of some substantial information, and they must have facts about where to operate, and some kind of analyses on which to base their major decisions as to the proper size of their installation and their scope of operation.

We have discussed elsewhere the recent focus of economic activity on the village of Massena and its environs, and while it is true that the initial boom of the Massena area will taper off considerably, the community is destined to become substantially more active as an economic center in the St. Lawrence area. On February 25, 1957, New York's Governor Harriman approved a contract between the Reynolds Metals Company and the New York State Power Authority by which 200,000 kilowatts of firm power[1] and 39,000

---

[1]The term "firm power" signifies power that is unrelated to the changes in the flow of the St. Lawrence River. "Interruptible power," on the other hand, is related to the variations in the river flow.

kilowatts of interruptible power were to be made available to the Reynolds Metals Company.

Massena, as a name, and aluminum have become almost synonymous terms. The ALCOA plant now located there is assessed at about $80,000,000. While not a gigantic operation when compared to other American industrial installations, it is the giant of St. Lawrence industry. It contains twenty-two miles of railroad and tweny-five miles of highway. The company-owned Massena Terminal Railroad shuttles approximately 30,000 cars per year and annual shipments have averaged in recent years more than 2,500 truck loads and 3,500 car loads. The establishment of the Reynolds installation will "aluminate" Massena a great deal more, for that company plans to build a reduction plant worth $88,-000,000 at Rooseveltown, which is just outside Massena. It is expected that the unfinished products of the Reynolds plants in Arkansas and Texas will be shipped via the St. Lawrence Seaway to Rooseveltown and there reduced into sheet aluminum.

The allocation of electric power to the Reynolds Company accounts for more than 27 per cent of the United States share of the total power output. Previously the Aluminum Company of America had contracted for almost 24 per cent of the total output of electricity by contract with the Power Authority in 1955. To produce one pound of aluminum takes approximately ten kilowatts of power. The present installation of the Aluminum Company of America already consumes more electricity than either the city of Syracuse or Rochester, including both residential and industrial uses. The power consumption by the aluminum industry in the Massena area will thus be immense, and amount to somewhere in the neighborhood of 50 per cent of the total United States share of the power produced at the Barnhart Island installation.

The Aluminum Company of America operation in Massena already employs about 6,000 persons. When the Reynolds factory is in operation, however, the number of factory employees will be increased by at least 1,000. The Reynolds Company will thus become one of the most important employers of labor in the St. Lawrence area. But this does not at all indicate the extent of the growth process in this particular community, for there is envisioned an arrangement under which the aluminum produced at the Reynolds plant will be further fabricated in the community of Massena. It will be made into automobile parts at a new General Motors plant to be built close to the Reynolds operation. The exact employment of the aluminum casting plant for the automobile industry is not yet known, but minimum estimates place the total employment at 500; maximum predictions place the employment far above that figure.

While these two new installations are the principal ones envisioned for the immediate location of Massena, it should be realized that their establishment will furnish impetus for many further changes and expansions in the economy of that part of the area and, indeed, the St. Lawrence area as a whole. Their influence as an economic stimulant will precipitate many extensions of economic activity that might be guessed at but at present could only amount to speculation.

It is helpful in analyzing the future potential of the St. Lawrence area to take some recognition of its normal growth pattern, from which it is at least somewhat illuminating to project what the future of the area might have been like without the addition of the contemplated new resources.

That is, what would the economic and business future of the area have been were not the Seaway and Power Projects emerging realities? One hears the term "underdeveloped area" often these days. Though the term is usually applied to places in the rest of the world, it is quite commonly applied to such locations as the St. Lawrence. The application of the term to the area here under study is valid enough as long as one does not mean by its use to infer that the area is an oppressed or depressed one for, as we have seen, the standard of living of people in the North Country is not especially low, even by high American standards.

Actually the economic life of the whole St. Lawrence area has been growing slowly, but steadily, even in the most recent past. It is not backward by any standard. It is neither one of complete stagnation nor of economic decline. On the other hand it is not an area in which there has been any very spectacular growth, for such growth as has taken place in the past decade does not equal the average advance throughout the whole of the United States. These characterizations are important in offsetting what lies at the basis of many predictions as to the future of the St. Lawrence area, i.e., the idea that its whole future rests almost completely on the new resources of the Seaway and Power Project alone.

One convenient index of the pre-Seaway, normal economic development of the area may be found in data concerned with power consumption. It is significant, for example, that between the years 1949 and 1954 in all three counties, St. Lawrence, Franklin, and Jefferson, the use of electric power in each of the categories of industrial, residential, commercial, and miscellaneous applications has slowly, but steadily increased, there being no decline in use in any one of the years indicated. (Figure I.)

59

FIGURE I

JEFFERSON, ST. LAWRENCE, AND FRANKLIN COUNTIES

Total Annual Electric Power Consumption
By Component Classes of Consumers 1949 - 54

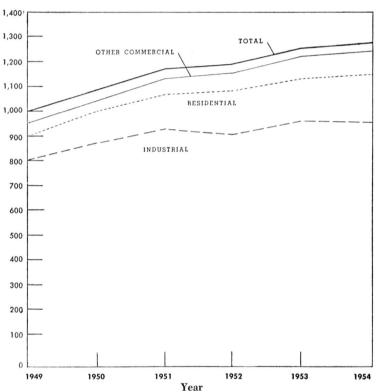

Source: S. Stanley Katz, "A Study of Electric Power Consumption in Jefferson, St. Lawrence and Franklin Counties, New York State" (unpublished Master's thesis, Syracuse University, 1956), p. 86.

60

FIGURE II

JEFFERSON, ST. LAWRENCE, AND FRANKLIN COUNTIES

*Total Annual Electric Power Consumption
and Population, 1949 - 54*

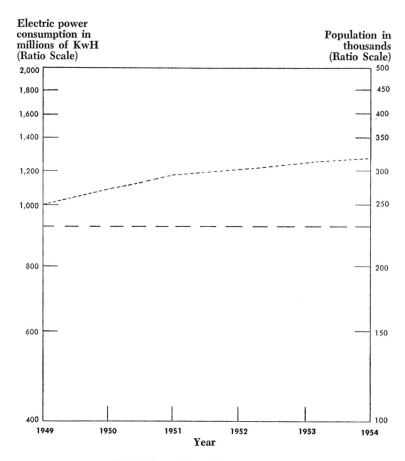

——————Electric Power Consumption

— — — —Population

Source: Based on **Sales Management, Survey of Buying Power** estimates
(S. Katz, "A Study of Electric Power Consumption in Jefferson, St. Lawrence, and
Franklin Counties, New York State," p. 89).

The rate of change of population as compared to the rate of change in power consumption is shown in Figure II. It can be observed that the population was virtually constant during the entire period between 1949 and 1954, but the electric power consumption increased from a billion kilowatt-hours annually to somewhere in the neighborhood of 1.3 and 1.35 billion kilowatt-hours per year. This is a clear indication that the use of electric power became much more widespread and more intense for industries, for trade in general, and for residential uses.

It is also significant that electric power consumption in the St. Lawrence has increased at a faster rate than disposable income, especially when one considers that the price level has shown a tendency to rise between 1949 and 1954. (Figure III.) Further, the rate of change of the manufacturing payrolls correlated rather closely with the increase in power consumption during the period in question (Figure IV), manufacturing payrolls increasing more rapidly than the use of industrial power during the period (Figure V). All of these various indices show clearly and illustrate the latent, inherent tendency for the St. Lawrence area to manifest at least some expansionary tendencies.

It is always difficult to project economic indices into the future. At best such crystal gazing is highly tentative, and it is always risky. However, we can make an estimate of the projected use of electric power for the three St. Lawrence counties in this instance with little fear that history will prove us wrong. The projection is for the period from 1955 to 1960 and is based on the assumption that the two new resource supplies, i.e., the St. Lawrence Seaway and Barnhart Island Power Project, will not be an influence, nor even be in the economic picture at all (Table IV).

TABLE IV

Projections of Annual Electric Power Demand
By Class of Consumer for Jefferson, St. Lawrence,
and Franklin Counties, 1955 - 1960
(In Millions of Kilowatt-Hours)

Class of Consumer and County	1955	1956	Year 1957	1958	1959	1960
Residential						
Jefferson	84.5	91.0	97.0	102.5	106.0	109.0
St. Lawrence	100.0	108.2	115.0	119.0	124.0	127.0
Franklin	25.5	27.0	28.0	29.0	30.0	31.0
Total	**210.0**	**226.2**	**240.0**	**250.5**	**260.0**	**267.0**
Commercial						
Jefferson	38.0	39.0	41.0	42.5	44.0	44.5
St. Lawrence	36.5	38.5	40.8	42.5	43.0	44.9
Franklin	14.5	15.5	16.5	17.0	17.5	18.0
Total	**89.0**	**93.0**	**98.3**	**102.0**	**104.5**	**107.4**
Industrial						
Jefferson	141.5	145.0	147.5	150.0	152.0	154.0
St. Lawrence	787.0	796.0	802.0	808.0	814.0	817.0
Franklin	31.5	33.5	35.5	36.5	37.0	37.5
Total	**960.0**	**974.5**	**985.0**	**994.5**	**1,003.0**	**1,008.5**
Total						
Jefferson	270.0	280.0	290.0	295.0	297.0	300.0
St. Lawrence	947.0	963.0	975.0	982.0	987.0	990.0
Franklin	83.0	90.0	96.0	100.0	103.0	105.0
Total	**1,300.0**	**1,333.0**	**1,361.0**	**1,377.0**	**1,387.0**	**1,395.0**

Source: S. Stanley Katz, "A Study of Electric Power Consumption in Jefferson, St. Lawrence, and Franklin Counties, New York State" (unpublished Master's thesis, Syracuse University, 1956), p. 110.

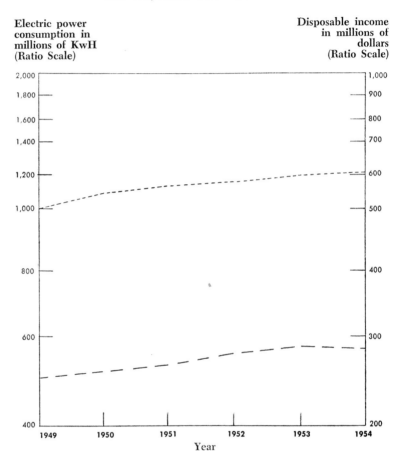

FIGURE III

JEFFERSON, ST. LAWRENCE, AND FRANKLIN COUNTIES

*Total Annual Electric Power Consumption
and Disposable Income, 1949 - 54*

Electric power
consumption in
millions of KwH
(Ratio Scale)

Disposable income
in millions of
dollars
(Ratio Scale)

——————Electric Power Consumption

— — — —Disposable Income

Source: Based on **Sales Management, Survey of Buying Power** (S. Katz,
"A Study of Electric Power Consumption in Jefferson, St. Lawrence and Franklin
Counties, New York State," p. 87).

64

FIGURE IV

JEFFERSON, ST. LAWRENCE, AND FRANKLIN COUNTIES

*Total Annual Electric Power Consumption
and Manufacturing Payrolls, 1949 - 54*

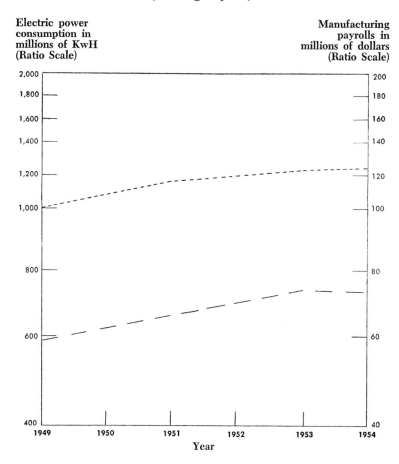

Source: Based on New York State Dept. of Commerce estimates (S. Katz, "A Study of Electric Power Consumption in Jefferson, St. Lawrence, and Franklin Counties, New York State," p. 88).

65

FIGURE V

JEFFERSON, ST. LAWRENCE, AND FRANKLIN COUNTIES

*Annual Industrial Electric Power Consumption
and Manufacturing Payrolls, 1949 - 54*

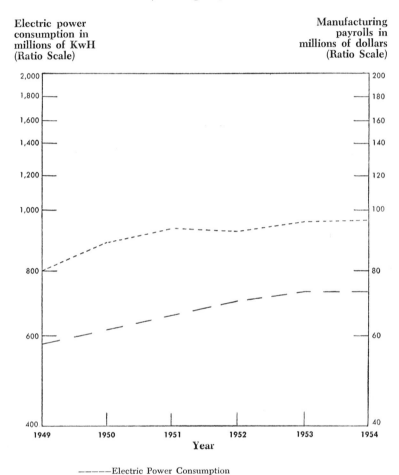

Electric power
consumption in
millions of KwH
(Ratio Scale)

Manufacturing
payrolls in
millions of dollars
(Ratio Scale)

Year

————Electric Power Consumption

— — — —Manufacturing Payrolls

Source: Based on New York State Dept. of Commerce estimates (S. Katz,
"A Study of Electric Power Consumption in Jefferson, St. Lawrence, and Franklin
Counties, New York State," p. 90).

This projection gives only the minimum probable requirements for the area. Such a future estimate, with respect to electric power, is merely one index to indicate that, if other things remained equal, there would be some substantial increases in this particular component of economic health as measured by disposable income and increases in the payrolls of manufacturing concerns. This argument is not intended to insist that electrical power consumption causes increases, necessarily, in the other two factors, nor that the other two factors always cause increases in the use of electric power. It is simply meant to assert that all three are interrelated parts of the basic structure of the St. Lawrence economy.

Without the Seaway and the Power Project development, the normal expected growth in economic life might very well have been accomplished without very much growth in population. Actually, the population structure might have become a more intense manifestation of the lopsidedness already mentioned. It would thus exhibit even greater tendencies to be weighted at the extremes of the younger and older age groups. This implies a lessening of the concentration of people in the twenty-five- to forty-five-year age bracket, because, without some such new element in the economy as the Seaway, the growth of the St. Lawrence area might not have become sufficient to hold these productive people in spite of some growth tendencies. After all, the American scene is a rapidly changing one and ever growing, and the normal process is that productive people are easily drawn away from the less active, stagnant, or slowly growing areas to those that are growing most rapidly. Projects such as the Seaway and power development are factors which help make and keep an economy dynamic.

The total capacity of the Barnhart Island plant will be just under two million kilowatts. While only half of this supply will be used in the United States, and the other half in Canada, it is perfectly clear that the normal growth in the economy of the St. Lawrence area could not begin to take up the power that will be created by the Barnhart Project for use on the American side of the river.

Of the capacity 940,000 kilowatts in the American share, 735,000 kilowatts are expected to be firm power. The remaining 205,000 kilowatts will be secondary and related to the fluvial changes which normally occur. Allocations of 174,000 kilowatts of firm power to the Aluminum Company of America, and 200,000 kilowatts to Reynolds Metals have been made, while the state of Vermont has been allotted 100,000 kilowatts, Niagara Mohawk Power Corporation 115,000 kilowatts, Plattsburg 30,000, and the Plattsburg Air Base 11,000. (Table V.) It is interesting to note that the contracts which have already been approved much more than cover the cost of the Power Authority bonds outstanding.

It appears at present, then, that somewhat over a third of the million kilowatts will be available for industrial use on the American side. But there will be more than 100,-000 other kilowatts which are coming in as a result of Niagara Mohawk investments in such places as Carry Falls, South Colton, etc. Thus it becomes clear that industry will shortly have available almost 500,000 kilowatts of new firm power from both public and private (Niagara Mohawk) sources. The "interruptible," that is, nonfirm power of the Barnhart project will be available for domestic use via the Niagara Mohawk system, and also directly to industrial users. The Reynolds Metals Company and the General

Motors operation are the first large and basic steps in the application of power from the new resource and thus the first great steps in the new development of the St. Lawrence area.

One could certainly enumerate many advantages of the area as a possible location for industry, but it is obvious that one of the them would be the availability of

TABLE V

Allocations of Power from The Barnhart Island Project in Kilowatt-Hours (June 1957)

Type of Use and Name of Consumer	Firm Power	Interrupted
Rural and Domestic		
State of Vermont	100,000	----------
Plattsburg Air Force Base	10,000	----------
City of Plattsburg, New York	30,000	----------
Village of Solvay, New York	12,000	----------
Village of Booneville, New York	3,800	----------
Rouses Point	2,000	----------
New York State Gas and Electric	20,000	----------
Niagara Mohawk	115,000	21,000
Miscellaneous Contracts, Unsigned		
But Negotiated	56,200	----------
Industrial		
General Motors	12,000	----------
Aluminum Company of America	174,000	65,000
Reynolds Metals Company	200,000	39,000
Totals	**735,000**	**125,000**

Source: New York State Power Authority.

power. It is not only a brand new element in the economic structure of the St. Lawrence country, but it is as surely an extremely important one.

Up to this point we have been considering only the immediate future of the North Country, but if we were to think of a period farther in the future, it becomes a fairly sound prediction that the successful operation of the Barnhart Island Project will intensify plans for future power projects in the general area. Thus the grand and immense resource we have been talking about in the Barnhart Project may be only the beginning of a vaster development and application of power in the area. Not only will new water sites for hydro plants be sought along the river, but thermal plants are likely to be considered. Whether they be coal, oil, or, what is more likely, nuclear plants, it is suggested that the endless supply of the St. Lawrence River water will be a great inducement for the location of thermal power establishments. Also the general location of the counties in the area, near sites of industrial importance, yet still far away from the great centers of population, make the area appropriate for certain types of nuclear development. In view of whatever validity there is in these predictions, one might well consider the Barnhart Island Project much more than just a power plant. It is actually the beginning of a great experiment in social engineering, for its success will undoubtedly lead to many different types of future development.

Water supply is another element of resource that is rich indeed in the area. Most American industry has for some time been finding it increasingly difficult to secure adequate water supplies to satisfy current needs and, with industry growing all the time, the water problem becomes more and more acute. Chemical and metal industries, and many others, are limited in their expansions by critical water availability. Thus the boundless water supply of the St. Lawrence River should stimulate the fertile imagination of the American businessman and technologist. Water, not only for power, but for industrial processes as well, will surely make the St. Lawrence region worthy of the investigations that are probably to be made by industrialists who are looking for investment possibilities.

The existence of a plentiful supply of power and water may also lead some to reconsider the usability of many of the mineral resources of the Adirondack Mountains. This might be true especially with regard to the iron ore deposits located there. Such basic considerations as these, when viewed in the light of cheap water transportation, may serve to attract industry into the St. Lawrence country.

But perhaps one of the greatest advantages of the area, given the new resources, is the great enthusiasm on the part of many individuals and communities in the North Country for further industrialization. There is intense desire in this direction, and it has already created a favorable industrial climate. The press, public officials, bankers, industrialists, and engineers are joined by the farmers, the working people, and the tradesmen in evincing a sharp interest in the economic future of the area and a deep appreciation of its possibilities. As we have pointed out before, there has been a tendency for both the future successes and the future failures of the area to be exaggerated and overemphasized, but these extremes are only evidence of the keen concern, on the part of the residents, with economic development. Such broad and intense desire for economic growth will be certain to become an advantage, since public attitudes play a

71

very significant role in commercial and business development.

With the advent of new establishments in the area, including even those industries which have a very high ratio of capital to labor, expenditures for wages, salaries, locally bought materials, etc., will be most likely to start an economic growth process which will both multiply the income of the area and accelerate the real investments. Primary effects of investment are, of course, important, but the many ancillary and secondary effects are of great importance in any growing and developing community.

A thousand new factory jobs in the aluminum reduction plant at Rooseveltown, plus another 500 or so in the General Motors foundry will probably mean more than 1,500 new jobs. The increase in personal, professional, and craft services will easily equal or might exceed the new factory jobs in number. Industries and firms serving the new factories, as suppliers, or serving as customers, will provide an unknown number of new jobs. At any rate, although the only two major investments in the vicinity are presently the Reynolds and General Motors installations, the gross investments surely will far exceed the capital necessary for those two single developments.

As important as water transportation is in many areas, modern industry is not likely to rely on it entirely. Water transportation is usually inexpensive and especially desirable for moving heavy bulky items when time is not a very important consideration. But there are many items of great value, and usually of light weight, the storage costs for which are high, and early delivery necessary. These items are best moved by rail, truck, and often air transport. The North Country contains a railroad network which is not at present strained and thus is in a position to carry more freight if additional demands were to be placed upon it. It is impossible to guess at this time just what auto roads will be required to support the future economy of the area, but there is a strong possibility that the present highway system might not meet the demands of developing industry. It is therefore probable that the road network will need considerable improvement and extension.

On more than one occasion in the recent past the target date for the completion of the Barnhart Island Power Project has been threatened by the inadequacy of the road system. The problem of highways is always paradoxical, for while it is true that roads attract industry to an area, no one knows exactly where to build and what roads to build until the demand actually exists. It is impossible at times to say whether the roads or the industries come first, since they are so closely interrelated. However, competent engineering studies in conjunction with industrial analyses should provide some insight and significant viewpoints which would be of value in state and local government plans for a satisfactory road system. Although at this point in the development it is impossible to be certain, it may well be helpful to the St. Lawrence area to provide easier access by road to New England, central New York, and eastern and western New York State as well. The major expansion of the system is chiefly the concern of the state and federal governments.

The Seaway will be of enormous importance to the iron and steel industry of the Middle West. But it may very well be that the Seaway also will signal the rebirth of the New York State iron and steel industry, for such a development is not at all beyond the realm of possibility.

As it is presently planned, the main purpose of the construction of the St. Lawrence Seaway is to connect the

Atlantic Ocean with the Great Lakes. This, in itself, obviously provides no very special benefits, economic or otherwise, to the St. Lawrence area, unless the existence of the Seaway will cause new firms to locate along its facilities. There is only a small fraction of New York's industry located along Lake Ontario and near its shores. What industries there are will probably be enormously affected. But the great industrial and trading sections of the state are not oriented at all toward Lake Ontario. All of central New York, with its hub at Syracuse, all of the southeast section with its hub at New York City, and also the very important industrial concentrations around Schenectady, Troy, and Albany, at the present time have no easy access to the Seaway and its advantages of low transportation costs.

For the past few years there has been some comment on the propriety of widening and deepening the Barge Canal from Troy northward. This 72-mile stretch of the Barge Canal is known as the Champlain Division and terminates at the north in the town of Whitehall on Lake Champlain. Lake Champlain, itself, stretches an additional 112 miles northward, and beyond the Lake is the Richelieu River, the rapids in which are by-passed by the Chambly Canal.

The waterway which exists at present is limited in use by the fact that its channel is at some locations less than 6.5 feet, and by the relatively small locks in the Chambly Canal. The total length of the Champlain Waterway is 263 miles. Between New York City and Montreal the Hudson River Canal route cuts the water distance from 1,671 miles to 450. Thus if a linkage between Montreal and New York City is decided upon, an inland water route already exists even though its capacity is severely limited.

Though the Hudson River, as an inland waterway, has been of very great importance to the northeastern part of the United States, its full potential is perhaps not yet realized. The Barge Canal system north of Troy is not extensively used at the present time. In 1954 the traffic over the entire Champlain Waterway was only 931,000 tons. There has been a slight increase in the annual traffic on this system since 1949, the greatest being the 80,000-ton increase from 1953 to 1954.

Fully nine-tenths of the total tonnage in 1954 was "through traffic"; that is, it originated outside the New York canal system and terminated its passage outside the system. By far the greater bulk of the local traffic consisted of the 65,000 tons of pulpwood moving from Glens Falls Feeder Dam to Glens Falls, which is a distance of only five miles. Petroleum products constituted the great bulk of the tonnage on the canal, accounting for over 90 per cent of the shipments.

Since the St. Lawrence Seaway has become an emerging reality, there has been a growing interest in creating a usable, efficient water connection between New York City on the south and Montreal on the north. Even prior to the commencement of construction on the Seaway, several bills had been introduced in the Congress of the United States to authorize the deepening and widening of the Champlain Waterway. There is considerable political interest and action in Canada on this very matter, and the legislatures of both Vermont and New York have shown much more than a passing concern over such a proposition.

There have been three alternative plans for providing a more usable water linkage. First, there has been proposed a 12-foot channel costing roughly between $25,-

000,000 and $30,000,000, most of which would fall on the Canadian government; second, a 14-foot channel to make the north-south waterway a depth equivalent to that of the New York Barge Canal. Such a channel, it is estimated, would cost between $90,000,000 and $130,000,000 with about two-thirds of the expenditure on the Canadian side. There has also been some talk of a 27-foot channel to make the Richelieu-Champlain New York canal of a depth equal to that of the St. Lawrence Seaway, costing an estimated $600,000,000 to $900,000,000, about three-fourths of which would be for work within the United States. Since most of the shipments over the canal at present are petroleum products, a pipeline to cover the route might be more feasible than a deeper and more efficient canal for all-around use. The high transshipment and warehousing costs involved would probably also preclude the shipping of newsprint and pulpwood over the canal if it were deepened. This is true because a good deal of the wood and wood pulp required for newsprint comes from areas that do not have ready access to the canal, and therefore would require a warehousing step in the transport process.

If the canal were to be rebuilt, it would have a definite impact on the economies of northeastern New York, Vermont, and southern Quebec. It would be well for someone or some agency to make thorough analyses of the potentials of the area with a reconstructed canal system, or with a new highway network as an alternative.

The St. Lawrence Seaway could conceivably be the key to the opening up of much of the area to the west, north, and east of the Adirondack Mountains. The economic future of the whole region, bounded on the south by metropolitan New York and the north by metropolitan Montreal, is related to some degree to the use found for the Seaway. If transport efficiency between these two centers were increased and costs reduced, the whole economic complexion of the St. Lawrence area would be viewed in a different light. A New York-Montreal tie is still a dream of the future, but the future has a way of quickly becoming the present.

Almost in the center of New York, halfway across the state on the Barge Canal from the city of Troy, which is the southern terminal of the Champlain Division of the New York State Barge system, is the city of Syracuse. Syracuse is located on the canal at the point where it enters Onondaga Lake, splits into two parts, one section running westward to Buffalo, and the other section north to Oswego on Lake Ontario—a distance of about thirty miles.

During World War II, metropolitan Syracuse entered a new phase in the development of its industrial makeup. Its population rose almost 16 per cent in the decade preceding 1950, and another 10 per cent by 1955. While most of the population increases took place in the areas immediately adjacent to the city, the rate of population and industrial growth in the whole metropolitan area is far greater than the rate of growth of northeastern United States. Interestingly enough, the city has grown mainly to the north, northeast, and northwest, and the industrial section thus seems to be edging its way in the general direction of Lake Ontario. Plans are at present afoot to develop an industrial area along the Barge Canal just north of Baldwinsville.

The city of Syracuse might eventually be made a lakeport by widening and deepening the short span of the canal between Lake Onondaga and Lake Ontario. Both Oswego and Syracuse would become, in effect, St. Lawrence

Seaway ports, and would supply an industrial and fabricating complement for present and for new industrial activity in the St. Lawrence area. Such a development would supply cheap water transportation without the necessity of transshipment. Furthermore, the entire United States industrial axis would be joined with the main Canadian industrial axis by a cheap water route to the Seaway. This problem, like that of the water route from New York to Montreal, should be studied carefully by United States and Canadian agencies.

There are, then, many possibilities in the area of transportation facility development, and, although the costs of some of these possible developments seem at first thought to be very great, in the long run the benefits received might prove them to be relatively small.

THE ST. LAWRENCE AREA
AND THE
CANADIAN ECONOMY

The general location of the St. Lawrence area is of very great importance to its future development. On the one hand it lies very near to the major axis of United States industrial activity, but, on the other, it is as close to the main axis of Canadian industry. As one views the industrial system of America it becomes apparent that there is a possibility that the Seaway and newly available power might well lead to the development of a spur from the main line of industrial development in the United States running north to reach and tap the resources of the St. Lawrence country. Inexpensive water transportation made possible through the deepening and development of the water route from the Atlantic Ocean to the Great Lakes contributes to the potential possibilities of rapid and broad economic growth in the area.

But there is much more to this argument, for if it is possible, or even probable, that the general flow of the American economy will spread to the area, it is just as likely that the Canadian economy, especially in view of its current rapid growth, might find it very advantageous to develop the St. Lawrence region. Such Canadian industrial development, of course, might center either on the New York side or on the Ontario-Quebec side, but in either case it would contribute to the general development of the whole area. This general prospect is not at all unlikely, since, in addition to the fact that the economy of Canada, like its counterpart in the United States, has shown a remarkable growth tendency, the industries that are growing most rapidly in Canada are those which are located very close to the St. Lawrence. Generally speaking, the major growth industries of the United States are much further distant and to the south and west of the St. Lawrence segment.

The economy of Canada has demonstrated remarkable developmental strength in recent years. A few comments on this strength and recent growth are pertinent to our analysis of the St. Lawrence Valley. The net value of Canadian production from all sources increased from $6,200,-000,000 in 1946 to $10,600,000,000 in 1950. This is an increase of almost 70 per cent. Some of the $4,400,000,000 rise is no doubt due to a general price increase, but even allowing for that factor to its fullest significance, this record is still one of very appreciable gain. Every industry in the entire economy showed an increase with the single exception of trapping. The greatest gains by far, though, were made in manufacturing and in construction.

Much of the industrial concentration of Canada is within the confines of the provinces of Ontario and Quebec. In the year 1950, for example, a good deal more than two-thirds of the gross value of all manufacturing production was accounted for by these two provinces alone. They led all other Canadian provinces in every phase of industrial output with the one exception of the production of wood products. British Columbia ranked first in that category, though the province of Ontario was second in rank, and the province of Quebec ranked third.

Ontario contains the main center of the heavy industrial production of Canada. The manufacturing of iron and steel products and transportation equipment amounted to more than two billion dollars in Ontario in the one year of 1950, while in the same year the province of Quebec produced over $1,300,000,000 worth of paper products, textiles, and clothing. Among the present leading industries of Ontario are motor vehicles, nonferrous metals, smelting and refining, iron and steel production, primary iron and steel production, motor vehicle parts, heavy electrical equipment, agricultural implements, and petroleum refining. The major leading industries of Quebec are nonferrous metals, smelting and refining, petroleum, and railway stock manufacturing.

In order to meet the growing industrial requirements for power, Canada has drawn heavily upon its water power resources (see Table VI for comparative provincial water power availability). Ontario Hydro-Electric increased its output by 1,400,000 kilowatts between 1945 and 1952. It planned to double its 1945 capacity by the end of 1956 or 1957. The rapid growth in demand and supply in Ontario is dramatized by the fact that since World War II, there have been put into operation no less than fourteen new hydroelectric plants. While the province of Quebec has experienced a less rapid growth in electrical production, it has nonetheless increased its power output, and sells some excess to Ontario. The United States industries and Ontario, in their turn, buy and sell power to each other as the occasion

81

requires. Such sources of extra supply, however, do not entirely meet the increasing need, and Ontario is in constant fear of a serious electrical shortage. Thus it is quite clear that the Barnhart Island Power Project, with its 940,000 kilowatts to be produced for Canada, is as important to the province of Ontario as it is to the St. Lawrence area.

While the capital requirements of the Canadian economy have been very great, much of the growth of its industry has in recent years come directly from domestic savings. Between the years 1946 and 1952 approximately

TABLE VI

Available and Developed Water Power by Province, 1 January 1955
Available 24-Hour Period at 80 Per Cent Efficiency

	At Ordinary Minimum Flow hp	At Ordinary Six Months Flow hp	Turbine Installation hp
Newfoundland	958,500	2,754,000	323,150
Prince Edward Is.	500	3,000	1,882
Nova Scotia	25,500	156,000	170,908
New Brunswick	123,000	334,000	164,130
Quebec	10,896,000	20,445,000	7,773,822
Ontario	5,407,000	7,261,000	4,845,486
Manitoba	3,333,000	5,562,000	756,900
Saskatchewan	550,000	1,120,000	109,835
Alberta	508,000	1,258,000	258,710
British Columbia	7,023,000	10,998,000	2,246,868
Yukon and N.W.T.	382,500	814,000	32,440
Canada	29,207,000	50,705,000	16,684,131

Source: **Canada, 1955,** Dominion Bureau of Statistics, Ottawa, 1955, p. 130.

$14,000,000,000 have been accumulated in long-term capital equipment investments, of which the net inflow of capital from outside sources amounted to only $1,200,000,000. Another billion dollars came from the reinvestment of profits gained from previously placed foreign investments, so almost 83 per cent of the fourteen-billion-dollar Canadian investment between 1946 and 1952 came from Canadian sources. During the period 1946-1953, the total long-term foreign investment in the Canadian economy was approximately 20 per cent of the net fixed capital formation. This is a vivid indication of the strikingly self-supportive nature of the economy of Canada.

The United States has been the chief supplier of capital from outside sources. (Table VII.) It may even be argued that most other nations are either neutral or a hin-

TABLE VII

Net Private Capital Receipts by Canada, 1946 - 53[1]
(In Millions of Canadian Dollars)

Source[2]	1946	1947	1948	1949	1950	1951	1952	1953	Total
United States	88	−164	111	64	961	554	−78	258	1,794
Sterling Area	−126	−33	11	−40	−75	74	−74	53	−210
Other Countries	2	−62	1	−33	31	5	−9	19	− 46
Total	−36	−259	123	−9	917	633	−161	330	1,538

[1]No sign indicates net inflow; minus sign indicates net outflow.
[2]By country of transmission.
Source: R. A. Radford, "Canada's Capital Inflow, 1946-53," International Fund Staff Papers, February 1955, p. 221.

drance to Canadian capital formation since many of them during recent years have been repatriating their Canadian investments. Yet, it should be pointed out, the Canadian-American relations with regard to foreign investment have been largely reciprocal, for while the United States supplies a good deal of investment in Canada, Canadian investment in the United States is also appreciable. It was only $846,-000,000 in the year 1952, but by 1956 it had increased to $1,500,000,000. Most of the increase, however, resulted from the reinvestment of profits gained by the firms of Canada that operate within the United States.

From the foregoing description one might suspect what is true of the Canadian economy as compared to that of the United States: the rate of increase of productivity of Canadian manufacturing is greater than in the American economy. The main reason for this difference is probably the newer equipment and the relative youth of Canadian industry. It has also not progressed so deeply into diminishing returns as has the older industrial system of the United States. It should be borne in mind, however, that we are not referring here to the *level* of productivity, but only to the *rate of increase* in productivity. The levels of productivity of industry in the United States are generally greater than any nation of the world has achieved. But Canada's rate of productivity has come to exceed that of America and is still increasing much more rapidly. For example, the value added by manufacture per worker in the United States, when measured in current dollars, increased in the years 1947-1951 by approximately 25 per cent, while the corresponding figure for the Canadian economy was over 45 per cent. Whatever else this might indicate, for the purpose of our analysis it would seem to demonstrate thoroughly that were Canadian know-how, Canadian efficiency, and Canadian managerial skill to unite with American labor skill and resources in the St. Lawrence area, a very strong economic productive instrument would be established.

Such a combination as here suggested is a very real possibility since the resources that are available in the St. Lawrence area for use in the United States domestic manufacturing enterprise are equally available, on either side of the river, to Canadian manufacturers. There would be a definite added advantage to some industries and firms if plants were on the American side of the river, since any tariff hurdles that are imposed by the United States would be avoided. This would be an advantage to any operation.

The proximity of the St. Lawrence area to the industrial axis of Canada is important for another reason to Canadian firms considering St. Lawrence area investment. Location there would tend to conserve Canadian managerial skill. The distances between the main industrial centers of Quebec and Ontario and the St. Lawrence region are very easily covered. Managerial staff could thus make frequent, even daily, personal contact between the home plant in Canada and a plant site in the United States.

These arrangements would be facilitated by the lack of ideological barriers between Canada and the United States. Resources, language, culture, attitudes, and basic points of view of businessmen are, for the most part, the same on both sides of the river; and consumers, farmers, and the people generally are but slightly affected by the boundary between Canada and the United States. Usually when adjacent or close national economies develop as rapidly as that of the United States and Canada both are doing in the industrial spheres, and as the national incomes increase, trade

85

relations between the two economies are enhanced and increased. This is not only true of raw materials and consumer goods, but producer goods and semifabricated items of all sorts become part of the mutual exchange.

What has been true of economic exchange in recent years is probably very significant in this respect. American imports from Canada averaged only about $350,000,000 per year between 1935 and 1938. But in 1950 and 1951 the average was above $2,100,000,000 annually. This is an enormous increase and can be accounted for partly by the fact that in the period 1935-1938, on the average, Canada was the source for only 13 per cent of United States imports, but by the 1950-1951 period this amount had risen to over 21 per cent, and continues to rise with respect to some items. (See Table VIII for some selected items.)

Likewise, American exports to Canada have increased remarkably. In the period 1935-1938 the United States exported, on the average, only $492,000,000 a year to Canada. By 1950-1951 American exports to Canada rose to $2,300,000,000 annually, which was an increase from 15 per cent to 19 per cent of the total United States exports. It should be pointed out that much of the goods which are imported from Canada into the United States must withstand tariff barriers of varying rates (Table VIII).

Since we have been implying right along that the St. Lawrence area and the Ontario region which borders on the St. Lawrence River are homogeneous in most respects, the reader might well have raised the question as to the reasons for the differences in the rates and amounts of development on the American and Canadian sides.

A good part of the explanation for the rapid growth of the Ontario side as compared to the slow growth of the

St. Lawrence area lies in the rather obvious facts of economic geography. The national economy of Canada has extended its industrial locations along the St. Lawrence River from Quebec through Montreal to Ottawa and along the shores of Lake Ontario and Lake Erie. Windsor, Ontario, is the western anchor of the main concentration of the Canadian industrial axis.

The main American industrial axis has one of its many anchors at Detroit, which is directly adjacent to Windsor, but, on the other hand, the eastern extension of the United States industrial axis is bounded by such sites as Niagara Falls, Buffalo, Rochester, Syracuse, and Schenectady. The American industrial axis does not extend north until it reaches New England's coastal plain.

While the Canadian industrial pivot is oriented to the area around Lake Erie, Lake Ontario, and the St. Lawrence River, the American axis revolves from the Great Lakes, but does not extend to the St. Lawrence River. A formidable barrier to migration, trade, and industry is posed in the Adirondack Mountains. In the United States, the general flow of goods east of the Great Lakes is largely by rail and by truck. For almost a century now it has not depended to any great extent on water transportation. In fact, in the earlier beginnings of industrial development, the Erie Canal (which was replaced by rail and road transport) was probably a factor in determining the northern geographic limit of the industrial axis of the United States in its New York segment.

Thus the expanse between the St. Lawrence River and the New York State Barge Canal has never developed into an industrial area. Nearly all of the region west of Lake Champlain and Lake George and north of the Barge Canal,

TABLE VIII

Major Imports from Canada, 1952 - 1954
Selected Items

	Range of Tariff		Value of Imports $000			
	Ad Valorem	Specific	1954	1953	1952	AVERAGE
Live Stock		1¢ - 2½¢ per lb.	13,267	10,179	2,758	8,735[1]
Meat Products	Free to 35%	Free to 3¾¢ per lb.	42,057	46,215	16,930	35,067
Fish	Free to 4%	Free to 1⅞¢ per lb.	60,151	63,035	66,920	63,369[1]
Raw Hides	7½% - 17½%		3,285	4,622	4,738	4,215
Leather		25¢ - $5.00	3,105	3,301	2,158	2,855
Leather Goods	5% - 40%	per dozen pair	2,104	2,305	1,916	2,108
Furs	Free to 37½%		19,888	17,203	19,506	18,866
Whiskey		$1.25 per gal.	51,242	52,228	44,544	49,338
Malt Liquor		12½¢ per gal.	4,385	4,065	2,958	3,803
Drugs, Crude	Free List	Free List	925	1,149	1,079	1,051
Drugs, Advanced	5%		919	1,595	1,185	1,233
Logs	Free List	Free List	11,052	12,641	13,178	12,290

88

Lumber		Free to 75¢ per 1000' board measure	223,260	207,857	193,294	208,137
Wood Products	Free to 30%		48,902	42,199	42,386	44,496
Pulpwood, Wood Pulp, Newsprint	Free List	Free List	824,564	814,901	793,552	811,006
Paper Products	Free to 22½%	Free to 4½¢ per lb. Free to 50¢ per lb.	13,515	16,354	17,015	15,628
Minerals and Metals	Free to 12½%	1½¢ per gal.	493,039	490,582	489,343	490,988
Chemicals	Free to 30%	Free to 25¢ per lb.	25,684	32,097	24,416	27,399
Fertilizers	Free List	Free List	45,717	45,671	44,500	45,296
Seeds		Free to 3¢ per lb.	9,389	9,696	8,805	9,297[1]
Grain	5%	4¢ - 21¢ per bu. 10¢ - 30¢ per 100 lb.	81,933	161,632	157,825	133,797[1]
Fodders and Feed	Free to 2½%	Free to $1.90 per ton	21,294	25,147	37,098	27,846
Fresh Fruit and Vegetables		⅜¢ - 3.7¢ per lb.	16,714	17,772	20,834	18,440[1]
Agricultural Equipment	Free List	Free List	60,095	66,878	94,476	73,816
Miscel. Manufactures	Free to 30%	Free to 2½¢ per lb.	74,310	79,092	74,691	76,031

[1]Quota.
Sources: U. S. Tariff Commission, **United States Import Duties, 1952** (As Amended); U. S. Department of Commerce, Bureau of the Census, **Report No. FT110, 1952, 1953, 1954.**

mountainous, rich in scenery, sports, and vacation sites, has been incorporated into the Adirondack State Park. It is virtually unimportant from the viewpoint of population and industrial location. The topographically beautiful, undulating country which borders the St. Lawrence River, and which runs along the eastern shores of Lake Ontario, has not lacked attractiveness for scenic sight-seers, but it has lacked the advantages of man-made resources to support either very much industry or a large population.

Canadian investment activity has also by-passed the St. Lawrence area, for it is largely motivated by the same rational factors as those which serve as the well-spring of investment in the United States. However, the recent development of the Canadian economy has been intense. The consequential great availability of investment funds, which is the hallmark of the economy there, in all likelihood will be continued for some time to come. The growing process in industrial enterprise does not lead to only larger and larger factories, and a more extensive geographic division. Success in any large-scale industry usually depends a great deal upon the development of a decentralized system of branch plants to gain all the advantages of special raw materials sources, markets, labor force, and other geographic factors. There are, of course, obvious disadvantages for any Canadian industry which seeks to expand its over-all output and scale of operation very rapidly in the limited Canadian market. The United States market in most items is many times the size of Canada's, and the former is one that Canadian managers wish to exploit, if possible. But a Canadian enterprise that looks to the American market for its main outlet is faced with the problem of the tariff, which is at times a controlling factor.

A perusal of the rather high tariff duties on products such as leather goods, preserves, footwear, plywood, and other wood products gives one some informative clues as to the types of firms that may profitably address themselves to the United States market in spite of the barriers the tariffs impose. Distance is no factor, for, as has been already pointed out, the St. Lawrence area is not far from the industrial centers of Canada. Such Canadian industry, therefore, which interests itself in the possibilities inherent in the St. Lawrence area developments, must face two basic considerations. It must first decide whether the Canadian market is big enough, or developing rapidly enough, to absorb any likely or possible increase in output, and therefore whether the move would really be profitable. Then, if it decides to move to the United States, it would be faced with the question of the propriety of locating at a site in the St. Lawrence area.

No definite and final answers can as yet be given to either the question of demand or that of location. One very important observation, however, can be made. Canadian firms, which already sell, or contemplate selling some or all of their products to the United States, have a clearly excellent opportunity to do even better if they locate in the United States. And there are sites within the St. Lawrence area that might well be considered carefully by such firms.

GOVERNMENT
AND THE
ST. LAWRENCE AREA

Since the population of the St. Lawrence area is scattered rather than concentrated, and since the concentrations that exist are not very great, a highly developed, specialized government structure has never taken shape. Therefore, the local governments are not important in the economic sphere, for their payrolls, their public works, and the economic effects of the local tax structures tend to be much less significant than they sometimes can be in the larger metropolitan communities. These facts apply to both county and town governments. The New York State and United States governments are destined to play important roles in the development of the area.

The Constitution, laws, and customs of New York have traditionally been opposed to offering special benefits as subsidy to attract industry. On the other hand the role of the state government is by no means either small or rigidly confined.

The pattern of the kinds of aid state and local

93

governments in the United States have given to encourage industrial development is one which shows wide variations. Some states, notably Arkansas, Delaware, Michigan, and North Dakota, allow new industries as many as ten years exemption from certain state taxes. In other states, local taxes are excused for a period of ten years to new firms, as in Maine, Louisiana, Michigan, and Delaware.

New York State offers new industry no special tax relief at all and has a policy of relying on the normal competitive forces to attract enterprises into the confines of its jurisdiction, and this restriction against tax relief applies to local governments as well. Such a system is a valid one, for to exempt a new firm from taxation really has the effect of adding to the burden of other taxpayers, both property owners and income receivers. This would inevitably lead to an inequitable distribution of tax costs in relation to benefits received. The "fly-by-night" firm, which comes into an area to take advantage of a tax exemption, but stays for only a short time, is a liability to all taxpayers. In a tax exemption system for business, as in the rest of life, one usually gets about what he pays for and, in the final reckoning, a price of zero usually gets the buyer a service worth what he paid for it.

In some communities, a low assessment is guaranteed a prospective new industry, but this is merely a subterfuge to cover up the more direct "give-away" of the exemption system. Such an approach is not used in New York State. Nor may the state's prestige and credit be used to back up local bond issues to acquire land, buildings, and equipment. A few states follow this latter practice regularly, including Alabama, Mississippi, and New Jersey. But this also represents unfairness since the resources of the state, which includes the entire population, are actually being made to support one firm.

The state of New York, however, does not have a tax exemption policy, but it relies, rather than on tax favors, on four other main principles. First, it has established a New York State Development Corporation, the function of which is to help new industry in the state become firmly established. New York is not unique in having such an agency, however, for Connecticut, Florida, Maine, Massachusetts, New Hampshire, Rhode Island, and Vermont all have established similar credit corporations to perform a kind of banking function for new and expanding industries. The law was passed under the administration of Governor Harriman in 1954, with considerable bipartisan support. The theory of the provision is that it will serve to supplement the already strong banking system of the state.

Secondly, the state undertakes a continuous program of business research, largely through its Department of Commerce, to determine as accurately as possible the resources and economic potential of the various areas of the state.

Thirdly, through both the Department of Commerce and through local governments, the state conducts an extensive publicity program to inform potential new investors of the resources of the state and of particular areas within it. This is a significant program and constitutes a major part of the work of the Commerce Department.

Finally, there are many state agencies, but most particularly the Departments of Commerce and Labor, that maintain educational and technical programs designed primarily to assist both business and labor in improving their proficiency. The Commerce Department cooperates with both public and private agencies in carrying out the publicity function, and, through the work of the Business Information Service, performs something of a combination research and publicity activity. By means of business clinics and seminars, and through technical advice, businessmen in any particular area are given the advantage of the knowledge and experience of technical experts drawn from business and government circles. This service is especially helpful to small businessmen.

The law also provides for local effort of this type. A county may appropriate up to 2 per cent of the previous year's budget to publicize its resources and advantages. In addition, any city, by state law, may make certain expenditures for making known the advantages of its locale. A city, however, with less than 50,000 inhabitants may not spend more than $1,000 annually, although Ogdensburg was permitted, by special action of the State Legislature, to spend $5,000 in the year 1955.

It is generally felt that one of the most important factors in attracting an industry to a particular area is a favorable site location in a generally advantageous area. Many of the larger firms in the United States employ sizable staffs only for the purpose of studying site locations and making market analyses, while many other firms contract special agencies at considerable expense to perform such work. There are many firms that can afford neither the maintenance of staffs for such research nor the expense of hiring it done. Yet these are precisely the firms that can afford least the risk of choosing a nonadvantageous site location. The New York State Department of Commerce attempts to meet this great problem for smaller business through the work of its Division of Economic Development and, at the same time, serves as an important complement to the research staffs of large industrial firms. This service of the Commerce Department can be of great aid in the development of an area such as the North Country.

Many local areas such as the towns, villages, and counties of the state can also use the services of the Department of Commerce, not only for assistance in the preparation of area analyses, but for assistance in general planning and zoning programs. The present attractiveness of any community is always important to its residents and to the business firms located in it. But continued attractiveness is of equal or even greater importance to a growing community. It is only through appropriate planning and zoning that present locational benefits can be assured continuation in the future.

In the case of general development of industry, the New York State Development Corporation will probably be of very great assistance. The hastened development of the St. Lawrence area will depend on the development of branch plants of larger concerns, but also upon the formation of new firms. Whatever new firms are established will probably not be industrial giants, although some industrial giants are likely to take up great quantities of power, when and as it becomes available. Firms employing 200 people or less, and medium-sized establishments will probably find it greatly advantageous to move into the St. Lawrence area. It is true that the New York State Development Corporation is not a state agency. It is a private agency, though chartered by the state, privately owned, and privately controlled. However, by its charter, it is devoted to the whole problem of assistance and supplying relief in financial undertakings for which the ordinary banking system might not always be equipped.

Assisted by the state and federal agencies, the Corporation will become an increasingly important resource in the development of the St. Lawrence region.

But there are many local groups of all kinds in the area that will also be of great assistance. The business climate and the general attitudes in the community are probably as important as any other consideration in attracting enterprise and holding it in the area. It is always difficult to make a start in industrial development, but when a start is made, the effect often becomes cumulative, and it tends to feed on itself. Local initiative and inspiration are important. Resources are important. Competent advice is important. Governments at all levels, universities, research organizations, and many informal organizations of varying character will no doubt have some part in the promotion of economic health and growth in the St. Lawrence country. Investment is not going to be made there merely as a favor to the people who live in the area. It will be made because the resources, the industrial climate, the facilities for economic activity, and the ways of community life are all conducive to investment, business operation, and a dynamic economic existence.

338.97S946n
The new St. Lawrence front[...]

T144 00120721 5

P R O V I N C E   O F

HIGHWAYS

RAILROADS

DIKES

POWER LINES

FORMER SHORELINE

0   2500 5000 7500 10000   SCALE IN FEET

0   SCALE IN MILES

PERGENTEAU
DIKE

KING'S HIGHWAY 2

LOCK 21

SAULT L

BE

CHRY

FARRAN'S
POINT

LOCK 22

INTERNATIONAL   BOUNDARY

CROIL ISLAND

LONG SAULT ISLAND

LONG SAULT
CANAL

OLD SOUTH CHANNEL

FORMER
RAPIDS

ALCOA
PLANT

CAT

FLOW

ST. LAWRENCE RIVER

DIKES
2 & 3

MASSENA

MUTTON RIDGE

DIKE

DIKE
4
DIKE

N.Y.C.R.R.

S T A T E   O F